THE NAME ABOVE ALL NAMES

GERALD C. LEWIS, SR.

THE NAME ABOVE ALL NAMES

DEDICATION

This book is dedicated to:
Java, for picking up all the pieces and putting them back together again.

And, to every reader searching for deeper meaning in God's Word, may your journey through God's Word reveal profound truths and lead to new understandings. As we embark on an extraordinary journey, may your relationship with God deepen, your love for Him grow, and your hunger for His Word grow stronger. Approach this book not for knowledge, but for an encounter with God. He knows you intimately and calls you by name. Listen very closely as the Holy Spirit unveils revelations through the sacred names explored in this book. It is my prayer that you'll never read His Word the same again.

Let's take a look, it's in the Holy Book!

With special thanks to Steven Jacobs,
Timothy Wright, Jr., and Bishop Michael Lee Loyd, II.

TABLE OF CONTENTS

INTRODUCTION

"Wherefore God also hath highly exalted him, and given him a name which is above every name: That at the name of Jesus every knee should bow, of things in heaven, and things in earth, and things under the earth; And that every tongue should confess that Jesus Christ is Lord, to the glory of God the Father." (Philippians 2:9-11, KJV)

What's in a name? Most modern readers of Scripture see biblical names as nothing more than just names—useful for identifying people and places, but with little to no additional meaning. However, just beneath the surface of each name lies a wealth of revelations that we often overlook.

To the ancients, a name captured an individual's essence, representing identity, reputation, character, personality, and purpose. Names also expressed a close relationship with God, as well as familial bonds. They even extract the essential and most important aspects of prophecy and meaning over generations. Our culture today, rarely recognizes the purposeful choice and profound significance of biblical names. But when we look beyond the lens of our 21st-century perspective, we realize how important names are in understanding key truths revealed throughout the Bible.

This book invites you to put aside the ideas we've absorbed from our everyday naming conventions and enter into the mindset of the biblical writers. *The Name Above All Names* explores the role of names in the Hebrew worldview, elucidating divine truths often missed in translation. We will examine the relationship between name and identity, purpose, authority, and God as depicted in the Old and New Testament. You will never look at the names in the Bible the same way again.

A name, like breath, expresses one's innermost being. Knowing someone's name gives you profound access to their identity. By looking at names from Adam to Jesus, we will see how Scripture uses these names to convey prophetic purpose and position, declare aspects of God's character, and reveal the natures of even the most seemingly insignificant people in the Bible. We will look at why names were sometimes changed and how knowing & using a name communicated authority and power.

The meanings of key Old Testament names provides new insight into who God will be, is now, and was in the past. From Genesis to Malachi, God gradually reveals His name. By the time Jesus makes His appearance in the Gospels, He has solidified an authority inextricably associated with His name. Jesus promises that His disciples will perform signs and wonders in His name. The book of Acts depicts this as coming true through the disciples. In Philippians, Jesus is proclaimed to have been *given* the name above all names. All of which has meaning for prayer, faith, and our relationship with God, which becomes clear as we dismantle our current understanding and notions of naming.

Contending for the Title of 'The Name Above All Names'

The Name Above All Names takes a one-of-a-kind journey through the vast landscape of divine naming, but with a specific goal in mind: to explore those exalted names that, within the intricate pattern of Biblical Hebrew and context, vie for the title of "name above all names." This exploration is not an exhaustive study of every name of God. Instead, it focuses on a carefully curated group of names that, due to their deep roots in Biblical Hebrew and their embedded significance within the Bible's narrative and theological fabric, have the potential to reveal the essence of God's ultimate identity and sovereignty.

At the heart of this journey is the understanding that names in the Hebrew tradition are more than just labels. They are full of meaning, including character, essence, destiny, and divine will. The Scriptures reveal every name of God, inviting us to a deeper understanding and relationship with the Divine. However, among the multitude of names, there are some that uniquely capture God's incomparable nature and relationship with creation, standing out as contenders for or illustrators of the supreme name that reigns above all.

Each name is meticulously examined using Biblical Hebrew—not merely as names but as windows into God's character and actions. This book focuses on the linguistic nuances, etymological backgrounds, and scriptural contexts that reveal the multifaceted nature of God's names. This approach allows us to appreciate the mind-changing ways in which these names express God's sovereignty, covenantal faithfulness, redemptive power, and eternal nature.

Furthermore, *The Name Above All Names* places each name in a larger biblical context, tracing its narrative significance from the Old Testament to the New Testament. This journey reveals the evolutionary trajectory of divine revelation, demonstrating how these powerful names not only reveal God's character and purpose throughout Israel's history but also how they come together in the person and mission of our Lord Jesus Christ. The titles and attributes bestowed upon God find their ultimate expression and fulfillment in Him, directing us toward the name that surpasses all others.

This exploration is based on the conviction that understanding these names in their original language and context can significantly deepen our relationship with God. It encourages the reader to engage with

Scripture in a contemplative manner, fostering a transformational encounter with the Divine as revealed through His names. Each name discussed in this book serves as light that illuminates God's self-disclosure, leading us to a more complete understanding of who God is and His salvific work in the world.

The Name Above All Names does not claim to fully reveal the inexhaustible depths of God's essence; no human work could aspire to such an accomplishment. Instead, it seeks to instill in the readers a deeper reverence and awe for the God who reveals Himself by name, fostering a more profound understanding of His transcendent majesty and imminent presence. This focused exploration invites the reader to ponder, worship, and eventually embrace the mystery of the name above all names, as revealed in the Scriptures and manifested in Christ Jesus, who is the nexus of God's redemptive love and power.

Whether you are well versed in Scripture or seeking to explore the Bible with greater depth, studying the Bible through the lens of the Bible will shed light on names in profound ways. It will add texture as you read through familiar stories, bringing them alive. You will uncover concealed insights into God's nature. And you will rediscover the power and intimacy inherent in the name above all names.

The Name Above All Names was written with the intent of immersing you in an interactive journey through the Scriptures. As you read each page, take the opportunity to bring God's Word to life by reading the verses mentioned in your Bible as you read each paragraph. Witness the Scriptures come to life, enriching your understanding and deepening your connection to our God through His Holy Book.

PREFACE

To truly understand the essence of the Bible, we must move beyond our modern Western perspective. Rediscovering the Bible as its ancient authors intended necessitates a thorough examination of the original Hebrew context of its names and words. This journey, encapsulated in the title "The Name Above All Names," delves into the profound connection between the ancient Hebrew language, its alphabet, pictographs, and the Hebrew culture.

Hebrew, unlike any other language, offers a unique way into the biblical text. Beyond its alphabetic structure, known as the Aleph-Bet, Hebrew incorporates pictographic elements and numerical symbolism. Each Hebrew letter, with its own meanings and forms, enriches the words it forms, conveying layers of spiritual truths and insights.

The Hebrew Aleph-Bet contains 22 consonantal letters that are essential to both the language and scriptural texts. These letters, written from right to left, have scriptural significance that goes beyond simple phonetics. These letters evolved from ancient pictographs, which were simple drawings that represented objects or concepts, to the standardized modern forms we know today.

Sir Flinders Petrie discovered the Proto-Sinaitic script at Serabit el-Khadim on the Sinai Peninsula in 1904–1905, providing invaluable insights into the origins of alphabetic writing systems. This script represented a significant evolution from earlier pictographic and hieroglyphic scripts in the ancient Near East.

Aside from their symbolic and phonetic functions, Hebrew letters also represent numerical values through "gematria." This numerical aspect enriches biblical texts with hidden meanings and patterns, allowing for better interpretation of divine truths encoded in scripture.

The Hebrew alphabet is expanded to 27 letters by including final forms for five letters, known as "sofit," when a letter completes a word. For centuries, Jews have preserved and revered their linguistic heritage, the Hebrew Aleph-Bet, which has shaped Jewish liturgy, scholarship, and daily life.

The Hebrew alphabet has final forms for certain letters, known as sofit (סוֹפִית), which are used at the end of a word. The final forms alter the appearance of the letters slightly. For example, ך (Kaf Sofit) is the final form of the letter Kaf (כ), which is pronounced similarly to the English "k." ם (Mem Sofit) is the final form of Mem (מ), pronounced similarly to the English "m." Similarly, ן (Nun Sofit) is the final form of Nun (נ), pronounced like the English "n." ף (Pey Sofit) is the final form of Pey (פ),

pronounced like the English "p." Finally, ץ (Tzadi Sofit) refers to the final form of Tzadi (צ), pronounced similarly to the English "ts." These final forms help to give the Hebrew script its distinct visual and phonetic characteristics.

Our investigation also delves into the Hebrew grammatical forms "qal" and "niphal". The "qal" form represents the simple active voice, which portrays direct action, whereas the "niphal" form represents the passive or reflexive voice, which frequently depicts receiving or being acted upon. These grammatical intricacies reveal deep theological and narrative nuances, emphasizing divine agency and human response in biblical narratives.

Throughout *The Name Above All Names*, we will look at Hebrew concepts that illuminate biblical names like Adam, Eve, Abraham, Moses, and Joshua. These names reveal profound truths about identity, calling, and divine purpose, providing glimpses into the Ancient Hebrew worldview and God's covenant relationship with His people.

The Bible's use of three languages—Hebrew, Aramaic, and Greek —serve different functions in conveying divine revelation. Hebrew meticulously describes historical and theological foundations in the Old Testament, whereas Aramaic, which is simpler and more direct, clarify truths in books such as Daniel and Ezra. Greek, which is precise and expansive, communicates Christ-centered teachings from the New Testament to a larger audience. This triadic use of languages spans millennia, bridging cultures and preserving the integrity of God's Word. Hebrew upholds biblical history and prophecy; Aramaic simplifies truths; and Greek explains the universal implications of salvation through Jesus Christ.

The Name Above All Names invites readers to discover the mysteries hidden within biblical names, revealing their transformative power in God's redemptive plan. May we grow in faith and understanding as we journey through Hebrew, Aramaic, and Greek texts, encountering the living Word—Jesus Christ, who bears the name above all names.

May our exploration of Scripture's languages illuminate our hearts and minds, bringing us closer to the divine author who speaks through every letter and word, revealing His eternal truth.

Order of Aleph-Bet	Hebrew Letter	Hebrew Name	Ancient Hebrew Pictograph	Ancient Hebrew Picture Description and *Symbol	Numeric Value
1	א	Aleph, Alef, El אלא - cattle (ox), yoke, learn	𐤀	Ox Head	1
2	ב	Bet, Beyt, Beth בת - house or tent	𐤁	Tent Floorplan	2
3	ג	Gimel, Gam גמ - gather, assemblage	𐤂	Foot *(Traveling or Journeying)	3
4	ד	Dalet, Dal דלת - a door	𐤃	Door to pathway *(Transition or Change)	4
5	ה	He, Hey הא - behold	𐤄	Man w/ arms raised	5
6	ו	Vav, Vau, Waw וו - tent peg, hook	𐤅	Tent peg/Nail *(Connection or Attachment)	6
7	ז	Zayin, Zan זן - hoe or mattock	𐤆	Mattock/Plough	7
8	ח	Chet, Cheth, Het, Heth חן - a wall	𐤇	Tent Wall	8
9	ט	Tet, Teth טיט - mud or clay	⊗	Basket	9
10	י	Yod, Yud יד - hand	𐤉	Arm and Hand	10
11	כ ך	Kaf, Kaph כף - palm / Khaf, Chaf	𐤊	Open Palm of Hand	כ 20 / ך 500
12	ל	Lamed למד - Teach	𐤋	Shepherd Staff *(Leadership or Guidance)	30
13	open מ / closed ם Spread Truth / Contracted Truth	Mem מים - Water	ᘱ	Water *(Life and Sustenance)	מ 40 / ם 600
14	נ ן	Nun נן - Seed of Seed	𐤍	Seed *(Life or Activity)	נ 50 / ן 700
15	ס	Samech, Samekh סמכ - to prop or support	𐤎	Thorn	60
16	ע	Ayin עין - an eye	⊙	Eye	70
17	פ ף	Peh, Pey, Pe פה - mouth	◡	Mouth	פ 80 / ף 800
18	צ ץ	Tsadeh, Tasade, Tsaddi, Sade צד - side	𐤑	Fish Hook/ Side	צ 90 / ץ 900
19	ק	Qof, Quph, Koph קופה - circle or revolution	𐤒	Sun of the Horizon	100
20	ר	Resh ראש - head	𐤓	Head of a man	200
21	ש	Shin שנ - tooth	𐤔	Two front teeth	300
22	ת	Tav תו - a mark	†	Crossed Sticks	400

Copyright 2024 ⓒ This chart may not be copied or distributed without written permission from GCLMEDIA, LLC.

Adapted for NAAN and Revised 41324

XIX

Chapter One

SHEM

What is your name? Do you know what it means? Most likely, your parents chose your name because they liked it, or maybe they named you after someone special. But more often than not, most of our names have no specific meaning, or if they do, we are unaware of it; our parents simply made them up. This may come as a surprise to you, but unlike many of our names today, names in the Bible were much more than just what someone was called; they were reservoirs of power and identity. Today, even the care and arduous lists of names that parents go through to choose a name for their newborn child do not come close to the ancient practice.

For the ancient Hebrew people of the Bible, naming someone was much more than just picking a name they liked for them. The name they chose purposefully captured the individual's essence and foretold their future. In their culture, the selection of a name revealed the person's identity, character, purpose, and place in the divine narrative. While in the same breath connecting the person to their lineage and their sacred bond with God, embedding prophecy and meanings that lasted a lifetime.

The names given throughout the Bible were also richly descriptive, each reflecting an individual's characteristics or significant life events. For instance, while Abram's transformation into Abraham reveals a shift in authority and his call into divine purpose, the name Adam exemplifies the idea of being "first" and means "mankind" or "man," while also revealing God's desire for humanity. In this light, the significance of names in Scripture reveals a realm of profound intimacy and relational depth. To know some name is to know them intimately. When God addresses Moses by name (Exodus 33:12) or Jesus calls His sheep by name (John 10:3), it transcends mere recognition and reflects a tender, deeply personal bond.

The numerous names attributed to God in Scripture—such as El Shaddai, "God the Nourisher," or Yehovahyireh, "The Lord Sees and Knows"—unveil His multifaceted nature, bringing us closer to understanding His essence.

Throughout the Bible, to use a name meant wielding authority, and acting "in the name of" meant to operate in the authority and power of the name spoken. This is made evident when Jesus empowers His disciples to act in His name, signifying that they are acting under His sovereign authority (Mark 16:17–18). Understanding this grants us more than just insight into Jesus' identity; it opens doors to the Kingdom of

Heaven. Hence, to say "in the name of Jesus" goes beyond that which is earthly and gives the believer divine access and favor.

We translate the English word "name" from the Hebrew term "shem," but shem is much more than just a name; it represents one's reputation, essence, and vital being—the breath of life within them. Amazingly, the word "neshamah," meaning "breath," vividly expresses this profound concept, by having "shem" ingeniously nestled right in the middle of its spelling. This revelation exquisitely illustrates the profound reflection of one's soul in a name, enlivened by God's divine breath. This seamless integration of "shem" at the very core of "neshamah" reveals the intricate design of the Hebrew language and the divine imprint on all aspects of our existence.

Neshamah נִשְׁמָה
Shem שֵׁם

Abigail's plea to David in 1 Samuel 25 serves as an eye-opening example of this. Her husband, Nabal, whose name means "fool," helps to illustrate the biblical concept of shem. After David and his men protected Nabal's flocks and shepherds from the rapacity of others in the wilderness of Paran, Nabal foolishly refused to show them any hospitality or gratitude. Abigail then plead to David, "Let not my lord, I pray thee, regard this man of Belial, even Nabal: for as his name is, so is he; Nabal

3

is his name, and folly is with him." (1 Samuel 25:25) Her plea highlights the belief that a persons name reflects and determines their personality and destiny. In Nabal's case, his name and foolish actions coincide, illuminating the inherent link between a person's name and the very core of their being. This link between a person's name and identity, character, and destiny, in many cases supported by divine influence, reveals the sacred and potent nature of names in the biblical narrative, identifying each as a divine imprint on the bearer's life and legacy.

The Power of a Name

The Bible is full of powerful names, each with allusions to the idea that it embodies essence, character, and destiny. Some of these names are even associated with significant life events, innate qualities, or promises from God. When God changes a name, as He did with Abram to Abraham or Sarai to Sarah, it represents a transition, heralding a new phase in their relationship with Him and emphasizing their roles in the unveiling of His divine plan. Jesus, too, emphasizes the power of names, instructing the disciples to approach God with reverence, as evidenced by "hallowed be thy name" in the Lord's Model Prayer (Matthew 6:9).

Hebraically, the act of naming is a deeply meaningful and expressive gesture that has the power to capture the essence of even life's trials and triumphs, as well as the hope that flows through them. The story

4

of Leah beautifully depicts this profound cultural practice in Genesis 29:31–35. Each name Leah chose for her sons—Reuben, Simeon, Levi, and Judah—is a compelling reflection of her pursuit of love, recognition, and, eventually, spiritual awakening.

Each of her sons' names expresses Leah's desire for her husband's affection, as well as her reactions to her situation. Reuben embodies Leah's yearning for recognition and love, signifying "See, a son" or "The LORD has seen my misery." Simeon, whose meaning is "The LORD has heard," symbolizes God's recognition of Leah's feelings of being unloved (hated). Levi, meaning "attached," represents her hope that childbirth will bring her closer to Jacob. Then, Leah had a life-changing revelation: God's gifts of her sons were more than just acts of compassion towards her; they reflected His inherent nature as the ultimate giver. This profound realization led her to name her fourth son Judah, which translates to praise. It was a pivotal moment in her spiritual journey, transitioning from yearning for her husband's affection to acknowledging God's limitless benevolence. Yet, just beneath the surface, the name Judah (יהודה) takes on an added significance, with it literally being the sacred four-letter name of God, YHWH (יהוה), with the insertion of the letter Dalet (ד). It symbolized God's intimate presence throughout her life, inspiring Leah to overflow with gratitude and adoration for His abundant blessings.

Leah's story unfolds as a narrative of personal growth and divine interaction, highlighting the Hebraic belief that a name is much more than just an identifier; it has the power to tell stories, convey deep emotional states, and even prophecy. Leah's decisions reveal not only her own journey from yearning to praise, but also the time-honored tradition of enshrining life's most profound experiences within the very names given.

The Hebrew term "shem" goes beyond the English concept of a mere "name," delving into a world where names and titles fuse together as one, emphasizing its profound significance. Did you know that the term "title" appears only three times in the Bible (once in 2 Kings 23:17 and twice in John 19:19–20), and none of them refers to a designation given to a person? Unlike English, Hebrew seamlessly integrates identity and title into the concept of "shem," rendering them indistinguishable. King David exemplifies this fusion, as his name "David," meaning "beloved," unites seamlessly with his royal title, depicting a ruler who is both authoritative and compassionate, mirroring God's heart. Sound familiar? (1 Samuel 13:14 & Acts 13:22) This linguistic depth challenges conventional wisdom, encouraging a greater appreciation for the multifaceted nature of identity and purpose encoded within a single word.

Although biblical names frequently had meanings related to significant life events or divine attributes, they provided insight into a person's role in God's plan. However, when translated into English, they often lose their depth of meaning, weakening the connection between the name and its divine or historical significance. Understanding names through the lens of Hebrew thought allows us to see them as manifestations of divine interaction and human destiny. They are more than just a means of identification; they also have the ability to influence and reflect their bearers' narrative journeys. The Bible is filled with names that encapsulate stories of faith, trials, and divine encounters, signaling us to delve deeper into their meanings and the stories they tell. Thus, *The Name Above All Names* is more than just academic; it is a journey to understanding the divine essence and the role of individuals in the grand narrative from creation to redemption.

As we journey through the pages of this book with the Holy Spirit as our guide, we will discover not only their etymology, but also the divine purpose and connection that each name represents. This exploration invites us into a deeper understanding of God and the profound story interwoven with each name, revealing the timeless bond between the divine and humanity encapsulated in the simple yet profound concept of "shem."

Blotting Out Names

Along with the power of a name, the biblical narrative intricately weaves the concept of "the blotting out of names" through stories of covenant, divine judgment, and ultimately redemption, painting a vivid picture of the consequences of sin while also offering the enduring promise of salvation to those who remain steadfast in faith.

In a powerful scene in Exodus 32:32, Moses stands as an intercessor for the Israelites after the Golden Calf disaster, offering himself as a sacrifice for their sin. He begs God, "If thou wilt forgive their sin, and if not, blot me, I pray thee, out of thy book which thou hast written." This moment not only underscores the seriousness of Israel's betrayal but also presents the idea of a divine ledger, a register that inscribes or expunges names according to their adherence to God's commandments. It is an allusion to the registering of the living and the erasing of those who die, as mentioned by King David in Psalm 69:28. A book that represents the sacred covenant that binds God to His people, with the erasure of a name indicating the ultimate separation from His grace and presence.

Deuteronomy 29:20 provides a stark warning against idolatry, deepening the narrative. Those who abandon the covenant in favor of false gods risk having their names blotted out from under heaven—a dire warning that covenant betrayal results in not only divine retribution but also complete erasure from memory, indicating a total breakdown in one's divine relationship, affecting both temporal blessings and eternal legacy.

Revelation 3:5 transforms the imagery from one of warning to one of hope, as Jesus assures the faithful in Sardis that "He that overcometh...I will not blot out his name out of the book of life, but I will confess his name before my Father, and before his angels." Here, the "book of life" shines as a beacon of eternal salvation and divine favor. Revelation, in contrast to the Old Testament's cautionary narratives, assures that those who follow Christ's teachings and overcome spiritual apathy will not only maintain their heavenly citizenship but also receive honor before the divine assembly.

This transition from a cautionary symbol to a testament of grace exemplifies the biblical journey from judgment to redemption. While the erasure from God's book of life was once a stark reminder of the consequences of forsaking Him, the New Testament reframes it in terms of the grace and redemption made available through Christ. Thus, the promise of eternal memory rather than erasure ensures their place in the heavenly realm and encourages believers to persevere in their faith.

The underlying idea of "blotting out a name" thus provides a profound exploration of the dynamics of faithfulness in the context of divine justice and mercy. From Moses' earnest plea and somber warnings in Deuteronomy to the hopeful assurances in Revelation, this pattern encourages the believer to reflect on their spiritual allegiance, emphasizing the critical importance of covenant loyalty and the joyful affirmation of salvation for the faithful.

As we delve deeper into the concept of "shem," known to us as "names," and the significance of names given throughout the Bible, leading up to "the name above all names," we are reminded of the life-giving breath that is blown into each one and its infusion into the soul, carrying whispers of the past, promises for today, and hope for an eternal future.

Chapter Two

THE NAME IN A NAME

In the human quest for spiritual understanding, few enigmas hold as much fascination and enlightenment as God's mysterious and most sacred name, YHWH. Within this name lies a depth that beckons those who dare to delve beneath the surface, leading them to the very core of God's existence. It serves as a bridge between the finite and the infinite, connecting humanity with the eternal. Also known as the Tetragrammaton (a Greek word meaning "four letters"), YHWH transcends mere letters; it embodies the essence of God, the plan for creation, and the manifestation of the life force that gives life to all that exists.

YHWH, with its ineffable power, encompasses both the means for understanding the divine and the essence that invites contemplation. It represents the paradox of our God, whose essence is the source of the never-ending becoming of all things, and who is both intimately known and infinitely beyond our comprehension. The sacred letters Yod, Hey, Vav, and Hey encode this divine name, written some 6828 times within the Old Testament, serving as a key to unlocking the mystery of existence itself, reflecting the tension between the known and the unknown, identity and manifestation.

As we delve into the depths of YHWH, we discover not only a name but a revelation—a testament to the dynamic interplay between the essence that defines existence and the tools we use to understand it. Human names straddle the line between inner identity and outward recognition, but the tetragrammaton displays the ultimate synthesis of essence and expression. This most holy name invites us to recognize the interconnectedness of all things and the divine spark inherent in every living creature's name.

What is God's Name?

In arguably the most pivotal moment in the sacred narrative of Exodus, Moses faces an existential question emblematic of humanity's search for divine understanding. Standing before the burning bush, Moses asks God a question that captures the anxiety of representation and the search for divine legitimacy: how should he introduce the God that is sending him back to Egypt? The response from God is profound and multifaceted, introducing two divine appellations that have piqued the interest of scholars and believers alike: "Ehyeh Asher Ehyeh," often translated as "I AM THAT I AM."

*"And Moses said unto God, Behold, when I come unto the children of Israel, and shall say unto them, The God of your fathers hath sent me unto you; and they shall say to me, What is his name? what shall I say unto them? And God said unto Moses, **Ehyeh Asher Ehyeh**: and he said, Thus shalt thou say unto the children of Israel, **Ehyeh** (I AM) hath sent me unto you. And God said moreover unto Moses, Thus shalt thou say unto the children of Israel, **Yehovah Elohim** (LORD God) of your fathers, the **Elohim** (God) of Abraham, the **Elohim** (God) of Isaac, and the **Elohim** (God) of Jacob, hath sent me unto you: this is my name for ever, and this is my memorial unto all generations." (Exodus 3:13-15)*

Did you notice the change? Why did God say His name was Ehyeh in one verse, but then instruct Moses to say Yehovah (also known as Jehovah or Yahweh, commonly rendered as "LORD" in English translations) sent me in the next? The answer lies in the Hebrew terms hayah (היה) and havah (הוה), which both mean "to be." Once you see this truth, you can't unsee it. In Hebrew, hayah (היה) is the past tense form of the verb "to be," indicating events or the existence of something in the past. Similarly, havah (הוה) is an ancient form of the same verb. Both hayah and havah convey the idea of "to be" in the past, but hayah (היה) is the more common usage, while havah (הוה) is the older, less common usage. Interestingly, when God instructed Moses on how to speak of Him, He used the less common form havah, implying a desire to emphasize His

13

timeless presence as the ancient, unchanging deity from the beginning—the one who brought all things into being. The structure of YHWH is future, present, and past. Yehovah has three syllabi: Ye, Ho, and Vah. Each relating to time is expressed in ye, as in yehiyeh, will be (future); ho, as in hoveh, is (present); and vah, as in havah, was (past). Thus, through this name, God reveals not only His eternal and self-sufficient nature but also bridges the divine-human divide with a name that will be a memorial to all generations.

Now here's a little Hebrew lesson: adding specific letters before a known term changes the tense. Prefixing Havah with the first letter of the Hebrew alphabet, Aleph א, transforms it into Ehyeh, meaning "I be," "I exist," or, in the King James Bible, "I am." When you prefix it with a Tav ת, it becomes "you exist," but when you use a Yod י, it becomes "He exists," the exact spelling of YHWH. Interestingly, just as Ehyeh expresses "I exist," Moses was to refrain from saying this to the children of Israel because, hebraically, it would be understood as Moses claiming to be "I am." Think about it. Moses said to God, "Behold, when I come to the children of Israel and say to them, the God of your fathers has sent me to you, they will ask me, What is his name? What shall I say to them?" If Moses had responded in the first person, Ehyeh, he would have identified himself as God. Instead, God, in His infinite wisdom, directed Moses to use the third person "Yehovah," which means "He exists" or "He is." If

14

the people asked Moses, his response would be Yehovah: "He is." This makes more sense when we take notice of the smallest of details given at the beginning, when God spoke His very first words recorded in the Bible, "Let there be light," which in Hebrew is yehi (יהי). At first glance, it is not obvious that yehi (יהי) is the imperative form of the verb hayah (היה). Therefore, it shouldn't be "let there be light," because God imperatively commanded, "Be light!" And there was light.

Havah הוה - To be | Hayah היה - To be

Ehyeh אהיה - I am / I was / I will be

Yihyeh יהיה - He is / He will be

Yehovah / Yahweh יהוה - He caused to be

As seen above, the first-person tense Ehyeh can be understood as "I am," "I was," or "I will exist," signifying the present, past, and future. Some very interesting instances in the Biblical narrative, such as Hebrews 13:8 and Revelation 1:8, intriguingly pick up this pattern.

In ancient Hebrew, "Ehyeh" is depicted through four pictographs:

- Aleph (א): 𐤀 the symbol of an ox meaning power, God the Father.

- Hey (ה): 𐤄 the picture of a man with his arms raised meaning breath, behold, reveal.

- Yod (י): 𐤉 Depicting a hand, meaning deed, finished work.

- Hey (ה): 𐤄 the picture of a man with his arms raised meaning breath, behold, reveal.

Together depicting God's breath and the work of His hands, Behold. This should remind us of Genesis 2:7. God was instructing Moses to tell them, "I am," He who created man and breathed life into his body, behold! I am the One who created everything, the God of Abraham, Isaac, and Jacob, and I will be with you. Tell them "He" sent you...

Revelations like this reveal profound truths about YHWH that go beyond the concept of a mere proper name, as we have traditionally defined it. YHWH is an epithet for the Divine, the Unnameable, the One whose essence and name are beyond our comprehension. Thus, among His people, compound names were formed by combining "YHWH" with another term to emphasize a specific aspect of God's character or actions. These compound names are more than just titles; they provide glimpses into God's multifaceted nature and dynamic interactions with humanity, revealing God is... the descriptor or action in question. They act as a divine mosaic, bringing together the various ways God manifests His presence, promises, and power in the lives of those He calls His own. Each compound name invites believers to explore the depth and breadth of God's essence, encountering Him as protector, provider, healer, and so much more. Each name serves as a testament to God's enduring and personal relationship with His creation.

16

This designation emphasizes God's transcendence by encapsulating His identity as the Creator of all things, the Self-Existing One, the Eternal—He who will always be, is, and was. With this understanding of God's nature it becomes explicitly clear that YHWH is not merely a name; it is an omnipresent force, deeply embedded in the fabric of existence and the essence of life.

How can we be so certain of this profound connection? In Acts 17:28, Luke gives a compelling testimony, saying, "For in him we live, and move, and have our being; as certain also of your own poets have said, For we are his offspring." This verse emphasizes the idea that our very existence, movement, and essence are only because of God's omnipresence and nourishment.

Furthermore, Psalm 145:3 proclaims, "The Lord is great, greatly deserving of praise, and His greatness is unsearchable." This verse highlights God's immeasurable greatness, emphasizing that His magnificence and the depths of His name are beyond our comprehension.

Together, these Scriptures highlight the astounding fact that YHWH represents far more than just a name—it represents the infinite, uncontainable essence of the Divine. In God, we find not only the source of our being but also the everlasting presence that sustains all life, inviting us into a relationship with the Eternal, the One who defies all of our attempts to name Him, even though He intimately knows each and every last one of us.

When we combine all of the ideas, concepts, and understandings we now have of YHWH, revelations begin to emerge from the Scriptures in ways that were not apparent before. John provides a perfect example when he writes, "Then the Jews said to him, Thou art not yet fifty years old, and hast thou seen Abraham?" Jesus said to them, "Truly, verily, I say to you, before Abraham was, I am." Then they picked up stones to throw at him, but Jesus hid himself and went out of the temple, passing through the midst of them." (John 8:57–59, KJV) Only what the Bible has already revealed to us can help us understand this verse.

Remember, "I am" is "Ehyeh," the name God gave Moses. So Jesus' response was truly, "Before Abraham was, "Ehyeh," or, to be more specific, "Before Abraham was, "I Existed." Jesus makes a clear and undeniable claim by stating this: He has existed since the beginning. Keep in mind that John is the author, and he begins his gospel with the same claim. "In the beginning was the Word, and the Word was with God, and the Word was God. The same was in the beginning with God. All things were made by him; and without him was not any thing made that was made. In him was life; and the life was the light of men." (John 1:1–4, KJV)

Once we recognize this pattern, we can see it repeatedly throughout the Scriptures. Keep in mind that YHWH represents time, or more accurately, timelessness, because God transcends time itself. YHWH is future, present, and past. It is clear that the author of Hebrews picked up on this pattern and continued it by writing, "Jesus Christ the same yesterday, today, and forever." (Hebrews 13:8, KJV) Isn't that mind-blowing?! Jesus is the same yesterday (past), today (present), and forever (future).

Substitutions of YHWH

The Tetragrammaton YHWH (the four Hebrew letters יהוה) is the most sacred name. Jewish traditions emphasize the ineffability and sanctity of God's name, leading to the loss of its exact pronunciation over time. This reverence led to the practice of not saying the name of God in public, while reading the Scriptures, or in prayer, instead replacing it with terms like LORD, Elohim, Adonai, and HaShem.

LORD

The tradition of substituting YHWH with "LORD" in English translations stems from Jewish tradition. Various English versions often render YHWH as "LORD" in all uppercase letters. This practice set YHWH apart from Adonai, the name spoken when reading YHWH aloud, but in written form Adonai uses the title case rendering of "Lord." This substitution aims to preserve the sacredness of the name YHWH while making the text more accessible and understandable.

Adonai

Adonai, which translates as "my Lord" or "my Master," refers to someone who has authority and power over others, a ruler. This name became a verbal substitute for YHWH in prayer and scripture reading, reflecting God's complete control over creation. When encountering the Tetragrammaton in text, Jewish readers frequently substitute "Adonai" out of reverence, recognizing the sanctity of the divine name by refraining from direct pronunciation. This practice demonstrates their profound respect for God's name and supreme authority.

HaShem

HaShem, which means "the Name," is the name used in everyday conversation, teaching, and when discussing the LORD in a non-liturgical setting. It functions as a circumlocution for the Tetragrammaton, allowing believers to address the LORD without using the sacred and unpronounceable name. HaShem emphasizes the Jewish tradition of reverence for the name YHWH, allowing us to speak of the LORD in everyday language while maintaining the holiness of the divine name.

The substitutions for the Tetragrammaton reflect a complex interplay of reverence, tradition, and practicality in Jewish religious practice and thought. They protect the sanctity of God's name while also making scripture and prayer accessible and meaningful to the faithful. This reverence for God's name, expressed through the use of these substitutions, emphasizes the depth of the Jewish people's relationship with God, which is based on respect, awe, and love.

Misunderstood Names of God

Many believers often misunderstand several of God's names, despite their profound meanings surpassing traditional beliefs. These misunderstandings are largely the result of linguistic and cultural barriers, as well as translational choices made in English Bibles. These names reveal God's multifaceted nature and His intricate relationship with us. Without diligently seeking a thorough understanding of the historical and cultural contexts in which these names were used, we risk overlooking their significance and fail to grasp their full implications, limiting our ability to appreciate the depth of God's revelation through these names.

Elohim

The very first of God's names revealed to us in the Hebrew Bible is Elohim, which has a wide range of meanings and connotations, making it one of the LORD's most intriguing and misunderstood names. The Hebrew term "Elohim" is a plural noun, and its meaning has been interpreted and debated, particularly in the context of monotheistic Judaism.

The Bible frequently uses "Elohim," typically meaning "gods" or "deities," to refer to the God of Israel—the Creator and Sustainer of the universe. This is evident in Genesis' opening verse ("In the beginning, God (Elohim) created the heavens and the earth."), which portrays Elohim as the all-powerful creator. Despite its primacy, Elohim's plurality has sparked much theological debate. Some argue that this plurality is a sign of majesty or supremacy, which ancient Near Eastern languages used to honor a single entity. This interpretation is consistent with Judaism's monotheistic doctrine, presenting God as singular while emphasizing His greatness and entirety of divine attributes.

Another interpretation of Elohim is that it represents God's all-encompassing nature, which includes all divine aspects and powers. According to this view, Elohim represents God, who embodies all divine forces and attributes and rules the universe with absolute sovereignty.

This interpretation of Elohim emphasizes God's multifaceted interactions with the world, including roles as creator, judge, protector, and provider.

Elohim, when viewed through the lens of its plurality as revealed in the "Us'" found in Genesis 1:26, Let "us" make man in "our" image after our likeness; (3:22) Behold, the man is become one of "us"; (11:7) Go to, let "us" go down; or, in Isaiah 6:8, who will go for "us?" represents the Divine Council in Jewish tradition or the Trinity in Christian theology. Genesis 18 further emphasizes this view of Elohim by depicting YWHW as three men appeared to Abraham. Through this view, Elohim can be read in the first person "Us," "We," or in the third person "They," if substituted for God.

For example:

*"In the beginning **"They"** created the heaven and the earth. And the earth was without form, and void; and darkness was upon the face of the deep. And the Spirit of God moved upon the face of the waters. And **"They"** said, Let there be light: and there was light." (Genesis 1:1–3)*

The use of Elohim in contexts involving divine judgment or creation sheds even more light on its meaning. Narratives in which God judges or creates frequently use the name Elohim, possibly to emphasize the authority and majesty of God's actions. This usage reinforces the concept of Elohim as a name that denotes God's kingship and sovereignty

23

over all creation. In his comprehensive commentary, the great Hebrew sage Rabbi Shlomo Yitzchaki, also known as Rashi, stated that "God as Judge created all things."

It's interesting to note that Elohim is the plural form of the name Eloah in Biblical Hebrew, unveiling a remarkable linguistic twist when it comes to depicting the Almighty. While Eloah spotlights the singular essence of the divine, reinforcing the core of monotheistic faith, its plural form, Elohim, dominates the text, ingeniously paired with singular verbs to signify one God. This intriguing play between singular and plural not only enriches our understanding of the divine but also paints a picture of God's layered and profound nature. Eloah appears only 57 times, primarily in the book of Job. Some of the most notable mentions are Job 3:4 and 12:6, as well as in Deuteronomy 32:15, Psalm 18:31, and Daniel 11:38, which each unfold the layers of God's unparalleled might and dominion, brilliantly illuminating the essence of monotheism with an awe-inspiring clarity.

The name "Elohim," when viewed through its plurality in the contexts of creation and judgment, intriguingly suggests a collaborative divine action. The Genesis creation narrative, notably using the plural forms "us" and "our" (Genesis 1:26), reveals the manifold nature of God as presented in Scripture. It emphasizes the plurality within the Godhead, later fully disclosed in the New Testament through the revelation of the Trinity: Father, Son, and Holy Spirit. The use of "Elohim" in conjunction with singular verbs further enriches this concept, blending the idea of God's singular essence with the diversity of persons. This multiplicity within the divine essence does not imply multiple gods but underscores the unified yet multi-personal aspect of the one true God, collaborating in acts of creation and governance, embodying perfect unity and diversity within Himself. The Hebrew Bible also uses Elohim to refer to all gods, including those of other nations, as revealed in, "Thou shalt have no other gods before me" (Exodus 20:3), adding to the complexity. However, when referring to the God of Israel, Elohim represents the singular, supreme God who possesses all divine authority and power.

El Shaddai

Did you notice the subtle revelation in Chapter One that the divine name El Shaddai means "God the Nourisher?" Many have understood "El Shaddai" as "God Almighty" throughout history, conjuring images of unparalleled power, might, and supremacy. However, Elohim and El Elyon convey the idea of omnipotence. Our understanding of El Shaddai as the Almighty God obscures the more nurturing aspects of God's essence, which "shaddai" reveals.

25

El Shaddai, when viewed through the lens of Hebrew, translates more tenderly as "God's breasts." Yes, you read it correctly! El Shaddai represents the divine essence of God's tender care, unconditional love, never-ending nourishment, and suffiuncincy. It causes us to clear our eyes and refocus on God as the ultimate nurturer, similar to a loving mother providing everything her infant needs directly from her breasts. Shaddai! In this likeness, El Shaddai sustains and nourishes all of His creation.

In Hebrew, the root word "Dai" means sufficiency. When prefixed with "Shin," it becomes "Shaddai," meaning "He who is sufficient." This profound interpretation is the foundation for the name El Shaddai, which reflects God's overwhelming ability to bless abundantly. In the biblical narrative, particularly in Genesis 17:1–2, this aspect of God's nature is critical because He promises to "multiply thee exceedingly." This promise is especially meaningful in the lives of the matriarchs Sarah, Rebekah, and Rachel, all of whom experienced barrenness. God revealed Himself to them, along with the patriarchs Abraham, Isaac, and Jacob, as El Shaddai, the One with the power to bestow fertility and abundance.

This divine epithet, El Shaddai, refers not only to physical multiplication but also to spiritual and material sufficiency. Genesis 35:11 encapsulates this concept with its imagery of blessings pouring forth like nourishment from the breasts, symbolizing sustenance and life-giving support. El Shaddai thus serves as a testament to God's ability to nourish, sustain, and multiply His people, emphasizing His role as a provider of all that is required for life and fulfillment. God uses the name El Shaddai to emphasize His role as the ultimate source of blessing and sufficiency in all aspects of existence.

God, as El Shaddai, cares for His creation with boundless compassion, embracing us with His warmth and life-giving sustenance. This profound truth highlights the significance of one of God's most overlooked aspects and invites us to see God in the likeness of a mother's tender embrace.

This profound truth should serve as a reminder that God is not only present in grand displays of power but also in love, gentleness, compassion, nourishment, and care. Does this remind you of the fruit of the Spirit? (Galatians 5:22–23) El Shaddai encourages us to recognize the strength of compassion and the mightiness of love in every nurturing act of our God—a name that reminds us that He is the ultimate nurturer who is always present, providing nourishment and love to all of us.

From Sufficient to Mighty

So, how exactly did El Shaddai come to be synonymous with "God Almighty"? This intriguing association is the result of a nuanced interplay of Hebrew words. While the "dai" in Shaddai traditionally signifies sufficiency, "shod" comes from the same root and means destruction. This linguistic pairing is poetically employed by Isaiah, where the use of destruction (שד, shod) alongside the Almighty (שדי, shaddai) creates a resonant echo that, while lost in English, is striking in Hebrew. This play on words appears again in Joel 1:15, cementing the connection between the terms.

Shod | Shaddai
Destruction | Sustenance
שד | שדי

The shift in the understanding of El Shaddai, "He who is sufficient," to "God Almighty" may have been influenced by a desire to clarify and elevate the concept of God's nature, especially given the potential confusion caused by the word "shaddai" being associated with "breasts." Genesis 49:25, which invokes blessings from the "breasts and womb," likely established this link, contributing to a more maternal imagery of provision and nurturing. Aligning El Shaddai with "God Almighty" served to emphasize God's omnipotence and authority, separating the divine character from gendered interpretations that could mislead or detract from a spiritual understanding of God.

This shift emphasizes a fundamental theological principle: God is Spirit, as stated in John 4:24, and transcends human gender characteristics. Despite presenting Himself in the masculine, God embodies characteristics traditionally associated with both genders, yet He remains unbound by either. Understanding El Shaddai as "God Almighty" eliminates any misconceptions about comparing God's nature to a woman or man, thereby reinforcing the concept of God's complete otherness and sovereignty. By emphasizing His infinite and all-encompassing nature, this theological clarity counters any simplistic or anthropomorphic views of God, including His ability to nurture, sustain, and protect His creation.

The nuanced meanings embedded within the Hebrew terms "shod" (destruction) and "shaddai" (sustenance) subtly illustrate a profound biblical theme of death and life, akin to the contrast between milk and meat. This linguistic pairing offers a deeper theological reflection on the dual aspects of God's interaction with the world: as both the destroyer of wickedness and the sustainer of life.

Together, these concepts encapsulate a cycle familiar in spiritual and physical life: just as in nature, where destruction makes way for new life, the biblical narrative suggests that God's acts of "shod" (destruction) clears the way for "shaddai" (sustenance). Scriptural symbolism reflects this cycle in the progression from milk to meat, where milk symbolizes the early, nurturing stages of spiritual life and meat signifies the more substantial, mature sustenance necessary for deeper understanding and stronger faith.

This interplay of death and life, destruction and sustenance, encourages believers to recognize and embrace God's entire nature. It implies that divine action in the world includes both ending what is harmful and nurturing what is good, demonstrating the divine balance required for humanity's spiritual development and survival.

Jealous God

Among all the intricacies of divine attributes one name that constantly raises eyebrows is "Jealous." When we come across verses like Exodus 20:5 and 34:14 in which God declares Himself to be a jealous God, it can cause confusion or even discomfort. How can we associate such a seemingly negative emotion with a perfect and all-loving being?

"I, the LORD thy God, am a jealous God." (Exodus 20:5b, KJV)

The fundamental meaning of this epithet reveals profound truths about God's nature, especially in light of His relationship with His people. At its core, God's jealousy refers to a sacred covenant similar to a marriage bond. A devoted spouse expects exclusive love and fidelity, just as God desires His people's undivided worship and allegiance.

God's jealousy is vividly depicted in Exodus 34:14, when He declares, "Thou shalt worship no other god: for the LORD, whose name is Jealous, is a jealous God." Here we see His possession of the worship and service that are rightfully His alone. It's not arbitrary or capricious jealousy, but rather a legitimate claim to what belongs to Him. Even Moses, the great leader and intermediary between God and His people, recognized this aspect of God's nature. In Deuteronomy 4:24, he emphasizes: "For the LORD thy God is a consuming fire, even a jealous God." This depiction highlights the intensity of God's desire for His people's exclusive devotion.

God's jealousy is not a passive emotion or insecurity but rather an active defense of His beloved. As a hen gathers her chickens under her wings, fiercely guarding her chicks from predators, God watches over His children, protecting them from the allure of false gods and the dangers of spiritual wandering. As Joshua warned the Israelites, abandoning the LORD for other gods invites His righteous judgment because "he is a jealous God; he will not forgive your transgressions nor your sins" (Joshua 24:19).

Understanding the two types of jealousy helps reveal the complexities of this divine attribute. God's jealousy over things that rightfully belong to Him demonstrates His sovereignty and exclusivity. His jealousy over those who choose not to belong to Him, on the other hand, stems from His commitment to protecting His people from spiritual harm and preserving His glory, as Isaiah eloquently declares, "I am the LORD; that is my name; and my glory will I not give to another, neither my praise to graven images" (Isaiah 42:8).

As a result, God's jealousy is not an imperfection but rather a reflection of His perfect love and commitment to His people. It invites us to affirm His supremacy in our lives, cultivating a relationship characterized by fidelity, closeness, and unwavering loyalty. The term קַנָּא qannâ' (jealous) refers to God's zeal and protection of His honor, highlighting His deep and pure love for us.

Jehovah-jireh

The faithful widely accept the name Jehovah-jireh, or more accurately in Hebrew, YHWH-yireh, as meaning "God will provide." However, this common interpretation actually limits the profound scope of its true meaning. Indeed, "Jehovah" refers to the sacred name of God, YHWH, whereas "jireh" is the Hebrew verb "yireh," which comes from raah (ראה) meaning "to see" or "to understand," with an added Yod (י) as the prefix, making it "He will see." The Bible beautifully illustrates the depth of this meaning when God presents animals to Adam and allows him to name them, a gesture that symbolizes observation and understanding rather than mere provision.

Abraham's narrative intensifies the poignancy of this nuanced interpretation. When Abraham lifts his eyes, he notices a ram caught in a thicket. Similar to God seeing which of the animals Adam would call his helpmeet, God observes Abraham to see if he would find the ram to be the necessary sacrifice. Such narratives highlight the essence of YHWH-yireh as more than just a provider but as a God who sees and understands deeply.

During Samuel's anointing of David, one of the most unlikely passages of Scripture further clarifies the richness of this name. God warns Samuel not to judge by appearances, saying, "For the LORD seeth not as man seeth (yireh); for man looketh (yireh) on the outward appearance, but the LORD looketh (yireh) on the heart" (1 Samuel 16:7, KJV). This passage vividly expresses how "yireh" conveys a profound seeing or understanding rather than providing. Despite Eliab's kingly appearance, the LORD saw into his heart, leading to His decisive rejection. The Hebrew term for "refused," mâ'as (מָאַס), conveys a strong sense of rejection or scorn. The writer's use of the term mâ'as reveals the depth of God's aversion to what He discovered while scrutinizing Eliab's heart. God's examination revealed Eliab to be fundamentally flawed and morally repugnant. Although this assessment may sound harsh, it is consistent with the LORD's divine ability to see and know beyond our appearances. The Scriptures constantly remind us of God's intimate knowledge of our hearts, which many people unwittingly acknowledge by saying, "God knows my heart." And He does; He sees, knows, and comprehends the essence of our beings, for better or worse.

This is not a new perspective; it dates back to Genesis 6, where God sees and knows the wickedness in humanity's hearts, prompting the flood. In Abraham's story, God's seeing and understanding are central themes. Abraham's declaration that "God will 'yireh' Himself a lamb for a burnt offering" (22:7) demonstrates a profound mutual understanding. If we read slowly and pay close attention to the narrative, God's seeing and knowing reveals one of the Bible's most powerful prophetic foreshadowings: God will see Himself a lamb, which He did through His Son, our Lord Jesus Christ.

Genesis 22:14 uses two forms of the Hebrew verb יראה to emphasize a profound revelation. While both instances are rendered in English as "Jehovah-jireh" and "LORD it shall be seen," their meanings differ. "Jehovah-jireh" reflects יראה in the qal stem, meaning "He shall

34

see," highlighting God's omniscience and foreseeability. In the phrase "LORD it shall be seen," יראה appears in the niphal stem as yeraeh, conveying "He will appear or be seen." This linguistic nuance reveals a deeper truth: YHWH not only sees, He will also reveal Himself on the mount.

Yireh (qal) | **Yeraeh** (niphal)

יִרְאֶה | יֵרָאֶה

He will see | He will be seen

For this reason, Abraham is referred to as God's friend, because he adhered to everything God commanded and believed everything God revealed to him, as Jesus affirms in John 15:14–15. The idea of God revealing the sacrifice of His Son, Jesus, to Abraham is subtly reiterated in Hebrews 11:19. Therefore, Jehovah-jireh goes beyond the simple interpretation of God as a provider, revealing a God who sees, comprehends, and sympathizes with the complexities of human hearts and circumstances. Similar to Hagar's encounter, in which she names God El Roi, Abraham prophesies that YHWH will provide a lamb for the sacrifice by revealing Himself on the mountain. This deeper understanding challenges us to recognize God's multifaceted nature, emphasizing His profound empathy and insight.

God's Rejected Names

The Bible records instances where God explicitly rejects certain names attributed to Him, underscoring the significance of comprehending and honoring the divine names He has selected. These moments underscore the significance of names in conveying God's true nature and the relationship He desires with His people.

Baali

The names we use to address God carry profound significance. We often don't even realize that there are divine rejections of certain names. Hosea 2:16 depicts one such rejection, illuminating an essential aspect of God's shem—character and desires. This rejection centers on the distinction between "Baali" and "Ishi," unraveling the intricate threads of meaning embedded within these words.

In Hebrew, the word "baali" holds a multifaceted significance. On the surface, it conveys the idea of a husband, but its deeper connotations extend to the realm of ownership and mastery. The Canaanite deity Baal, shrouded in fear and apprehension due to his role as a merciless master and pagan deity, epitomizes this duality.

The worship of Baal, with his titles like Lord of the Earth, Prince, and Lord of Rain and Dew, permeated ancient cultures, exerting a powerful influence over the hearts and minds of the people. Yet, for the Israelites, the association of God with the title "Baali" was not merely a linguistic matter, but a theological dilemma. It blurred the lines between the true God and the false gods of the surrounding nations.

In contrast, the rejection of "Baali" in favor of "Ishi" signifies a profound shift in the divine-human relationship. "Ishi," meaning "my man" or "my husband," reflects a more intimate and personal connection. It portrays God not as a distant and fearsome master but as an approachable companion, a loving partner in the covenant relationship with His people.

The encounter between Jesus and the Samaritan woman at the well, as recorded in John 4, beautifully encapsulates this transformation. Jesus transcends the religious and cultural barriers of His time, inviting the woman to move beyond her cultural and traditional notions of worship. She revealed that she has had five husbands (ba'alim), and the husband (ba'alakh) she is with now is not her own. In doing so, He unveils the essence of true worship—a relational connection with the Father, characterized by intimacy and authenticity. The five husbands the woman had were the five books of the Torah, and the husband, the rule, the guide, and the master she had now in Samaritanism was not her own.

As God beckons His people to call Him "Ishi" instead of "Baali," He invites us into a deeper understanding of His nature and desires. He yearns for a relationship based on love, trust, and mutual respect, where His people acknowledge Him not as a distant deity to fear but as a loving husband to cherish.

By rejecting the title "Baali," God reaffirms His dedication to a covenant of love and fidelity with His people, beckoning them into a relationship characterized by intimacy and communion. It is an invitation to embrace Him not as a distant dominating master but as a loving husband, ever-present and faithful in His care and provision.

Loammi

The name Lo-ammi, derived from the Hebrew "לא עמי," literally translating to "not my people," is bestowed with profound theological depth in the book of Hosea. Rather than a name God rejects for Himself, it symbolizes a pivotal moment in the divine-human relationship where God articulates the severe consequences of Israel's rebellion and idolatry. This naming in Hosea 1:9 underscores a painful declaration of

38

disownment, reflecting the chasm that has emerged between God and His chosen people due to their unfaithfulness.

Yet, the context surrounding Lo-ammi is not merely punitive; it is also a reflection of divine sorrow and an appeal to repentance. In naming Gomer's son Lo-ammi, God vividly illustrates the broken covenant between Him and Israel, signifying a temporary disassociation as a response to Israel's actions. This act is not God's abandonment but a profound call to reflection and change, a reminder of the consequences of turning away from the covenantal relationship established with Abraham, Isaac, and Jacob.

The subsequent narrative, however, reveals a deeper layer of God's redemptive plan. The declaration "for you are not my people, and I will not be your God" is not the end but a pivotal point leading to restoration. Hosea's prophecy later unfolds with promises of reconciliation and renewal, where "not my people" will once again be called "my people" and "not loved" will be called "loved." This transition from Lo-ammi (not my people) to Ammi (my people) encapsulates God's relentless pursuit of His people, despite their betrayal.

The reference to "Ehyeh," echoing the divine name revealed to Moses at the burning bush, serves as a powerful reminder of God's immutable presence and faithfulness. Despite the momentary declaration of "I will not be your God," implied in the name Lo-ammi, the covenantal name Ehyeh (I AM) reassures that God's essence remains unchanging and His commitment to restoration and relationship endures.

Therefore, Lo-ammi embodies a paradox of divine justice and mercy, a testament to God's willingness to enact judgment while simultaneously holding open the door to reconciliation. It invites introspection and renewal, offering hope that rejection can transform into restoration and separation into reunion under the covenant of God's everlasting love and faithfulness.

The Concealed Names of God

Unbeknownst to many believers, the Bible contains several names of God that are subtly concealed, woven into the fabric of the Scriptures in ways that are not immediately apparent. These hidden names contribute to our understanding of the Divine by revealing aspects of God's character and authority through cryptic references and allusions. By deciphering these veiled names, readers are invited to delve deeper into biblical texts, where uncovering each name becomes an act of discovery, revealing God's multifaceted nature. This journey through Scripture reveals hidden layers of meaning while emphasizing the profound mystery and majesty of the Divine presence.

Aleph

The Hebrew letter Aleph (א), spelled אלף–Aleph, Lamed, Pey, stands as the first letter of the Aleph-bet, rich in symbolic depth and spiritual significance. As a silent letter, its presence is profound yet understated, embodying the essence of beginnings and the unity that underpins creation. Numerically valued at one, Aleph represents the fundamental concept of oneness, reflecting the monotheistic core belief in the singularity of God. This oneness extends beyond mere numerical value, delving into the unity and indivisibility of the divine essence.

Aleph's shape, comprising two Yods (י) and a diagonal Vav (ו), suggests a spiritual bridge between the upper and lower realms, heaven and earth, hinting at the interconnectedness of all aspects of existence. Its silence in pronunciation speaks volumes, symbolizing the ineffable nature of the divine, a reminder of the mysteries that transcend human comprehension.

Beyond its individual meaning, Aleph is a gateway to deeper layers of understanding, encompassing concepts such as "Aluf" (master or chief), signifying God's sovereignty; "Ulfana" (teacher), reflecting divine wisdom; and "Pala" (wonderful), pointing to the miraculous aspects of God and His creation. Aleph thus emerges not merely as a letter but as a profound symbol, inviting contemplation of the divine and the unity of all things.

As we read the Bible, there are times when names were concealed, especially those tied to God. These instances serve as a thematic thread that highlights the profound mystery and sacredness of a name. This approach not only emphasizes the boundaries of human understanding but also elevates the divine-human interaction to a realm beyond a mere appellation, emphasizing reverence and the ineffable nature of the divine.

The story of Jacob wrestling with the mysterious figure at Peniel, as recounted in Genesis 32:29, presents one of the earliest biblical instances of this idea. During this enigmatic night-long struggle, Jacob asks his opponent for his name, only to receive a question, "Why is it that you ask my name?" This response, devoid of a direct answer, signifies the moment as a profound encounter with the divine, beyond human comprehension. Instead of revealing His name, He renames Jacob Israel, marking a pivotal transformation in his life and highlighting the encounter's sacred ambiguity. Jacob's essence and destiny shift from that of a heel-grabber who struggled with his brother in the womb to that of Israel—one who struggles with God.

The Book of Judges (Chapter 13) reveals another significant instance, where Samson's parents, Manoah and his wife, encounter an angel who foretells Samson's birth. Curious about the identity of their visitor, Manoah inquires about his name, only to receive the enigmatic reply, "Why askest thou thus after my name, seeing it is secret?" (Judges 13:18). The word "secret" here comes from the Hebrew term פלא "Pala," which means something wonderful or beyond ordinary understanding, reinforcing the narrative motif that divine beings—and by extension, the name—is viewed in mystery, emphasizing the transcendence and the human-divine boundary. Also, to know His name carried a weight of expectation, conveying an authoritative like anticipation for Him to respond when called. When you call someone's name they must acknowledge and answer the call. Why was it critical that Monoah knew his name? Why didn't the angel tell him? He did, but we cannot see the revelation until we read Pala backwards.

Aleph | Pala
פלא | אלף
Pala (Wonderful) is the obverse of Aleph

HaShem

The Tetragrammaton, YHWH, is the most sacred name of God in the Hebrew Bible, encapsulating the divine essence and ineffable mystery

43

of our Creator. The deep reverence and awe with which the masses regard it has led to a loss of its exact pronunciation over time. The reverence for the Tetragrammaton has led to the substitution of various euphemisms, the most common being "HaShem" (השם), which translates to "The Name." Jewish tradition deeply roots this practice, reflecting a profound respect for the divine name and its sanctity rather than being a matter of linguistic preference.

The renowned Jewish historian Flavious Josephus, in his work Jewish Wars 5.5.7, stated that the Tetragrammaton consists of four vowels. Many believers have assumed that the first Hebrew letter in YHWH Yod (י) is pronounced as "ee," the second letter Hey (ה) as "ah," the third letter Vav (ו) as "oo," and the fourth and final Hey (ה) as "ay." When combined, they produce sound "ee-ah-oo-ay," which gives rise to the name "Yahweh." However, it is important to note that Josephus did not explicitly state that the name of the LORD is four "vowel sounds." Given this, I believe Josephus was referring to God's name's sonorant quality, which suggests a resonance or melodic character.

In this book, I've chosen to use only the four letters YHWH to refer to the divine name due to the complexities surrounding its pronunciation and the variations found within its 6828 uses in the "Leningrad Codex." The Codex presents us with 10 variations of YHWH,

44

distinguished by 7 different vowel points, which have led to various pronunciations. These can be broadly categorized into four groups: YeHoVaH, YeHVaH, YeHoViH, and YeHViH, resulting in 2 primary vocalizations—YeHoVaH (6522x), YeHoViH (306x), with a third within Babylonian texts YaHWaY known as the English YaHWeH (3x). Given the range of variations and the reverence due to this sacred name, to maintain accuracy and respect, I have chosen to adhere to the original Hebrew representation seen in English as YHWH. Through this approach I seek to not only acknowledge His name's sanctity but also sidestep the complexities and debates over its correct pronunciation, focusing instead on YHWH's extremely profound significance within the biblical text.

The ancients' strong desire to uphold the Third Saying, "Thou shalt not take the name of the Lord thy God in vain" (Exodus 20:7), led to the substitution of YHWH for HaShem. Judaism's sages and scholars interpreted this commandment to mean that uttering God's sacred name outside of a holy context is considered disrespectful. To avoid inadvertent misuse of the divine name, "HaShem" emerged as a respectful alternative, preserving the name's sanctity while still allowing the faithful to refer to God in prayer and discourse.

Furthermore, the use of "HaShem" serves as a constant reminder of God's transcendence and immanent nature. While God is beyond human comprehension and naming, He is also deeply present in the lives of the faithful. "HaShem" represents more than just avoiding the sacred name; it embodies the Jewish view of God as infinitely mysterious and personally accessible. It emphasizes the Creator's relationship with His creation, which is characterized by reverence, love, and an ongoing quest for understanding.

What amazes me most about HaShem is the linguistic and conceptual parallels with Moses, Israel's great prophet and leader. The Hebrew letters "HaShem" (השם) flipped reveal "Moshe" (משה), just like "Pala" (פלא) and "Aleph" (אלף), which is intriguing. This fascinating correlation is more than just linguistic play; it reflects profound theological and symbolic connections.

Moses, as the intermediary between God and Israel, plays an important role in communicating God's law, presence, and promises to His people. We can interpret the inversion of "HaShem" to resemble "Moshe" as a symbol of God's reciprocal relationship with humanity. Moses communicated God's words and will to the people and then brought the people's prayers and yearnings before Him. Moses facilitates the dialogical nature of the divine-human relationship, with a focus on "HaShem."

This symbolic inversion also emphasizes the Torah's role as the Word of God—a manifestation of "HaShem" in the lives of Jews. The Torah, like Moses, serves as the conduit through which "HaShem" is known, loved, and revered. The Torah, then, becomes a living encounter with "HaShem," just as Moses was a human encountering with the divine. The remarkable linguistic representation of "HaShem" and "Moshe" enriches this tradition by revealing the complex relationship between the divine name, the Torah, and Moses' pivotal role. The sacred yet accessible name "HaShem" invites believers to delve deeper into God's mystery, presence, and word.

Moses | HaShem

משה | השם

These examples collectively demonstrate a key biblical motif: the transcendence of the divine and the inherent limitations of human understanding. The Bible communicates the vastness of the divine mystery and the reverent awe with which we should approach it by concealing certain names. This thematic element serves as a constant reminder of the divine's enigmatic nature as well as the role of faith in navigating the sacred mysteries. The refusal to reveal names in these stories does not signify an absence but rather an invitation to deeper contemplation of the divine's immeasurable and ineffable essence, which transcends human comprehension and categorization.

Father

In Hebrew, "Ab" (אָב), which means "Father," is a profound designation for God, encapsulating the depth of the Creator's relationship with His creation. This name, while simple, has layers of theological and relational significance, influencing the Judeo-Christian understanding of God. The use of "Ab" to refer to God goes beyond mere nomenclature; it represents an intimate, personal, and authoritative relationship, emphasizing God's care, guidance, and protection for His people.

Many will be surprised to learn that in the Old Testament we find the first mention of God as "Father." Although in many cases it is not so easily seen, the Old Testament designation of God as "Father" is valuable, highlighting a distinct aspect of God's relationship with His people. Unlike the more commonly used names "Elohim" or "YHWH," which emphasize His sovereignty, power, and creative authority, the title "Father" adds a deeply personal and relational dimension to God's character.

In the Old Testament, the title "Father" ascribed to God unveils a profound layer of divine intimacy and care lavished upon Israel, His chosen people. This designation is more that just a title, it is deeply relational, mirroring the loving, protective, and guiding bond shared between a father and his children. A striking instance of this relational depth is found in Exodus 4:22, where God instructs Moses to tell Pharaoh, "Thus says the LORD, Israel is my son, my firstborn." This declaration subtly but powerfully implies that if Israel holds the esteemed position of God's son, then, by divine extension, God stands as Israel's Father. The use of "Father" to describe God goes beyond mere terminology, embodying His unwavering commitment to nurture, guide, and protect His faithful in the same way that a father would his children, demonstrating God's divine compassion and care for His people.

One of the most notable instances of God being referred to as "Father" is in Isaiah 63:16, where the prophet declares, "Doubtless thou art our father, though Abraham be ignorant of us, and Israel acknowledge us not: thou, O LORD, art our father, our redeemer; thy name is from everlasting."

The name "Father" is a moving recognition of God's enduring relationship with His people, going beyond even the foundational figures of Abraham and Israel (Jacob) and emphasizing God's role as both progenitor and redeemer.

Similarly, in Jeremiah 3:19, God expresses His desire for Israel to return to Him by saying, "Thou shalt call me, My father; and shalt not turn away from me." God expresses His desire for a reciprocal relationship with His people, characterized by filial loyalty and affection.

The sporadic use of referring to God as "Father" in the Old Testament highlights the evolution of this concept in the New Testament, where Jesus frequently addresses God as "Father," inviting believers into a more intimate and personal relationship with God. The Old Testament's more formal and distant titles, replaced by Jesus' intimate and personal address, mark a significant shift in our understanding of God's nature and relationship with humanity.

Thus, the occasional use of the name "Father" for God in the Old Testament lays the groundwork for the complete revelation of God's fatherhood in the New Testament. It serves as a link between God's covenantal promise of care and protection for Israel and all believers' open invitation to have a close, personal relationship with God as their Father through faith in Jesus Christ.

Jesus' teachings, where He repeatedly refers to God as "Father" in His prayers and teachings, highlight God's desire to be addressed as "Father". Although referring to God as Father is not a new revelation, it was a radical departure from traditional Jewish practice, which frequently used more formal titles for God. Jesus uses "Father" to address God, emphasizing the personal relationship He has with God and inviting His followers to view and interact with Him in the same intimate way. Through Jesus, addressing God as "Father" becomes an invitation to recognize and embrace God's close and personal bond with humanity.

Furthermore, Jesus' command to call no one else "Father" on earth, recorded in Matthew 23:9, emphasizes the exclusivity and sanctity of this title for God. This directive does not forbid the use of the term in familial or respectful contexts, but rather emphasizes God's unparalleled spiritual authority and fatherhood. It emphasizes the idea that, while earthly figures may hold positions of authority or paternity, the ultimate Fatherhood belongs to God alone, who is the source of all life, power, and wisdom.

The term "Abba," an Aramaic word for father, adds to this concept. Jesus used "Abba" in His prayer in the Garden of Gethsemane, conveying an even deeper sense of intimacy and trust, similar to "Daddy" or "Papa" in English (Mark 14:36). This name, while denoting affection and closeness, also implies obedience and submission, as evidenced by the extended meaning, "Father, I will listen." It depicts a relationship marked not only by love and intimacy but also by reverence and a willingness to submit to God's will, capturing the dual aspects of affection and sovereignty inherent in God's fatherhood.

The use of "Ab" and "Abba" to refer to God as Father exemplifies God's unique, intimate, and authoritative relationship with His followers. It is a relationship that defies human comprehension, encompassing the ideal balance of intimacy, care, authority, and adherence. Jesus encourages us as believers to approach God with the confidence and love of a child for their father, fully relying on His guidance, protection, and provision. In doing so, we recognize and honor God's unique position as the ultimate Father, whose fatherhood is perfect, eternal, and all-encompassing, providing a model of obedience, respect, and love that informs and transforms their relationship with Him and one another.

In his letters to the Romans and Galatians, the Apostle Paul uses the term "Abba" to refer to believers, signifying their adoption into God's family through the Spirit of Christ. Romans 8:15 says, "For ye have not received the spirit of bondage again to fear; but ye have received the Spirit of adoption, whereby we cry, Abba, Father." Similarly, Galatians 4:6 states, "And because ye are sons, God hath sent forth the Spirit of His Son into your hearts, crying, Abba, Father." In these passages, "Abba" becomes a cry of the believer's heart, expressing both intimate familiarity with God and willing submission to His authority and guidance. Just as a father hears the cry of his children and runs to see, so too does our Heavenly Father (Genesis 18:20–21, 21:17, Exodus 3:7-8, and Judges 6:7–10). The Holy Spirit invites believers to partake in Jesus' intimacy and submission to the Father, affirming their position as God's children and heirs to His kingdom.

Each use of "Abba" in the New Testament emphasizes a posture of humility and dependence on God. It reveals a deeply personal and committed relationship with God, marked by trust, love, and a willingness to follow Him. This dual sense of intimacy and submission encapsulated in "Abba" provides a powerful model for Christian discipleship, encouraging believers to approach God with the openness and trust of a child, completely reliant on His wisdom and providence.

The biblical use of "Abba" encapsulates the essence of believers' relationship with God, characterized by deep love, trust, and submission. Christ invites us into an intimate family relationship with God, allowing us to freely express our deepest fears, hopes, and desires, all while remaining committed to His perfect will and sovereign plan.

Concealed Within Ab

The name "Ab" (אָב) is deeply symbolic, representing a strong leader of the house. It depicts authority, guidance, and protection, all rooted in ancient Hebrew society's patriarchal structure, in which the father was both the head and the heart of the family.

Amazingly, within the word "Ab," an inherent numerical significance emerges—Hebrew letters are also used as numbers, and here, the letters Aleph (א) and Bet (ב) combine to reveal the number three. Aleph, the first letter in the Hebrew alphabet, represents unity and has a numerical value of one. Bet, the second letter, represents duality and has a numerical value of 2. Together, as "Ab," they lead to three, representing a progression from unity to multiplicity and implying the multifaceted nature of God's provision, care, and leadership.

This numerical unveiling within "Ab" subtly reflects the theological depth of the Scriptures, where the concept of three reveals completeness and divine perfection, as seen in God's triune nature (Father, Son, Holy Spirit). Thus, "Ab" expresses not only a familial role but also the comprehensive and multidimensional aspect of divine leadership and care.

Understanding a name reveals the essence of its bearer, including their identity, attributes, and character. It's like peeling back layers, with each name providing a deeper insight into the person who bears it. This is why God is known by so many names; each one reveals a different aspect of His being, unveiling more about His nature with each revelation.

Chapter Three

NAMES IN GENESIS

The book of Genesis introduces us to God as well as a number of noteworthy people, such as Adam, Eve, Noah, Abraham, and Sarah. As prototypical representations of humanity, the names of these key figures carry weight and significance, revealing important truths about human identity, purpose, and relationship with God.

The First Man and Woman

Adam, which means "man" or "mankind" in Hebrew, is the first person the Bible introduces to us. However, Adam is not a proper name, as many of us might have traditionally believed. Instead, it is an epithet that emphasizes not only his status as the progenitor of the human race (the first man), but also his God-given authority over the Earth. In Hebrew, he is referred to as HaAdam, where Ha means "the" and Adam means "man," crowning him "the Man." As the Genesis narrative continues, the LORD God creates animals and brings them to the Man, just as a father brings a bride down the aisle to meet her groom. One by one, He brought every beast of the field and every fowl of the air to see what the Man would call (קרא qârâ') them—that is, to see which he might "accost" to be his helpmeet. However, the Man did not choose any of the living creatures presented to him to be his helpmeet. So instead, whatever the Man called them became the "name" of that living thing.

- Kelev (כֶּלֶב) - Dog: The Hebrew word for "dog" is "כֶּלֶב" (kelev). While on a surface level, "kelev" is simply a dog, there's an interesting interplay of words found within its name that relates to the dog's characteristic loyalty and companionship towards humans. "Kelev" can be broken down into "כֹּל" (kol, meaning "all") and "לֵב" (lev, meaning "heart"), suggesting that a dog is "all heart".

- Ari (אריה) - Lion: The Hebrew word for lion, "ari" (אריה), is associated with strength and leadership. The lion is often seen in biblical and Jewish tradition as a symbol of power, courage, and majesty, representing the tribe of Judah and the city of Jerusalem in Jewish symbolism.

- Tzvi (צבי) - Deer: The Hebrew word for deer, "tzvi" (צבי), conveys grace and beauty. In the biblical context, deer are often symbols of swiftness and grace. The imagery of a deer is used in the Scriptures to describe beauty and also the longing for spiritual connection, as in the thirsting of a deer for water.

56

- Dvash (דבורה) - Bee: While "dvash" means honey, the word for bee in Hebrew is "devorah" (דבורה), which interestingly shares the root with the word for speaking or words. This connection might hint at the bee's industrious nature and its role in the ecosystem as pollinators, essential for the flourishing of life and the sweetness it brings through honey, which is often associated with pleasant words and wisdom in Jewish literature.

- Shachaf (שחף) - Seagull: "Shachaf" is not just the Hebrew word for a seagull but also shares a root with the word for longing or yearning, possibly reflecting the seagull's constant search and its freedom over the vast seas. It captures the bird's essence as a wanderer of the skies and seas, embodying freedom and the endless quest for sustenance.

- Nachash (נחש) - Snake: The word "nachash" for snake can evoke the creature's cunning and stealth. In biblical narratives, the snake is often associated with temptation and cunning intelligence, such as in the story of Adam and Eve. The essence of the snake as crafty and wise, capable of both harm and healing (as in the symbol of the Nehushtan), is embedded in its Hebrew name.

Eve

Similarly, Adam's act of naming his helpmeet and counterpart represents an important point in the history of humanity. Initially, the narrative refers to the first humans as the Man and the Woman, emphasizing their roles as Iysh and Ishshah rather than individual identities. In Genesis 3:20, Adam names his wife Eve, which comes from the Hebrew word Chai חי, meaning "life" or "living." This act of naming her is significant because Eve is recognized as "the mother of all living." Adam not only gives her a personal identity, but he also emphasizes her central role in the formation and continuation of human life. This moment emphasizes the importance of names in conveying essence and purpose, capturing the full scope of Eve's contribution to humanity's story.

And Adam called his wife's name Eve; because she was the mother of all living. (Genesis 3:20, KJV)

The Name Man and Woman

The Hebrew word for "man" is "איש" (Iysh), and "woman" is expressed as "אשה" (Ishshah). Upon closer examination, we uncover an intriguing linguistic nuance: each term carries a unique letter not present in the other. This subtle distinction emphasizes the unique but interconnected nature of man and woman in Hebrew.

58

Iysh איש | Ishshah אשה
Man - י | Woman - ה

The Hebrew words for "man" (אִישׁ, Iysh) and "woman" (אִשָּׁה, Ishshâh) share unique letters, revealing a profound connection. These letters form "יה" (YH).

Consider this: the letters "יה" (YH) from the divine name YHWH pose an interesting question. Are they just a short form, or could they mean something more? Could "Yah" be a proper name of God and not just an abbreviation, or maybe a digram made up of the first and second letters of YHWH? Alternatively, it could serve as an acrostic, with "Yah" representing the first and last letters of the divine name. Even in just two letters, the enigma of God's name remains, inviting deeper contemplation.

Is Yah the First and Second, or the First and Last?
YHWH or **Y**HW**H**

Interestingly, removing the divine component (יה, YH) from both "man" and "woman" reveals אֵשׁ (êsh), which means "fire." This implies that man and woman, on their own, are like fires with the potential for infinite consumption. However, when man and woman unite, it represents the joining of two powerful forces, each with its own distinct energy and characteristics. The presence of Yah (יה) brings them together and

59

transforms them into something greater, symbolizing a "one flesh" unity enriched and guided by the divine. This unity (echad) leads to:

- Synergy and Intensification: Just like when two fires merge and intensify, when a man and a woman come together, their combined energies can create a synergy that amplifies their individual strengths, passions, and desires. Together, they may achieve more than they could alone, fueling each other's ambitions and dreams.

- Emotional Explosion: the meeting of a man and a woman can lead to an emotional explosion of sorts. This could involve intense feelings of love, passion, and connection that ignite rapidly when they come into contact with each other, leading to a deep and profound emotional bond.

- Mutual Growth and Support: Similar to how one fire may suppress another by consuming its oxygen, when a man and a woman come together, they may provide mutual support and encouragement, helping each other grow and flourish in various aspects of their lives, whether it be spiritual, personal, professional, or emotional.

- Spread of Influence: When a man and a woman unite, they can also contribute to the spread of their influence and impact on the world around them. Together, they may inspire and empower others, igniting positive change and making a difference in the lives of those they encounter.

Just as with fire, when a man and a woman come together, it's essential to nurture and maintain the relationship, fostering a healthy and harmonious connection built on respect, communication, and mutual understanding. Yet without Yah the two alone just burn.

Again, the figure traditionally known as "Adam" in English versions of the Bible is referred to by the Hebrew term "אדם" (âdâm), rather than a personal name which broadly translates to "human-being" or "mankind." This designation signifies the LORD God's intention to represent the first human as the foundational essence of humanity itself. In naming the woman "Eve," the man is recognizing her as the "mother of all living," yet he himself is implicitly understood as the "father of all living" through the generic term adam. This absence of a specific name underscores a profound connection between humanity and the Divine, highlighted by the direct dialogues and interactions with YHWH, God's unpronounceable name that encompasses His eternal and self-existent nature. Thus, the narrative doesn't merely recount the origin of individual beings but illustrates a primordial figure's central role in the unfolding human saga, intertwined deeply with the divine purpose and the broader tapestry of creation.

The narrative then shifts as Eve becomes a mother, naming her firstborn son Cain, or "Qayin," which comes from the act of acquiring or creating, symbolizing her role in bringing forth life with the help of the LORD. Cain's name, derived from Hebrew "קָנָה" (qanah), represents creation, possession, and even provoking jealousy. It also has an unexpected connection to cattle rearing.

Abel, whose name means "transience," and interestingly appears only briefly before Seth is introduced. Seth, named after the word "appointed," represents a divinely appointed successor to Abel, demonstrating how names in these accounts convey deeper meanings and destinies.

Similarly, Lamech's declaration when naming Noah, "He will comfort us in the labor and painful toil of our hands caused by the ground the Lord has cursed" (Genesis 5:29), emphasizes the rest and comfort that would come through him, highlighting the anticipatory role that names play in expressing hope and purpose in the midst of adversity.

These early biblical narratives show that names, deeply rooted in their Hebrew origins, contain significant insights into identity, purpose, and divine interplay, providing a profound understanding of the people they represent.

Noah

Noah's name, derived from the Hebrew "Noach" (נֹחַ), holds significant meaning in the biblical narrative, representing rest, comfort, and a new beginning for humanity. The origin of Noah's name is intricately linked to his role, as articulated by his father, Lamech, in Genesis 5:29. Lamech's declaration reveals the dual essence of Noah's name and destiny—the promise of relief and consolation in the midst of humanity's hardship, which seems to have far worsened since the curse pronounced on the Earth.

The name "Noach" comes from the Hebrew verb "nacham" (נחם), which means "to bring relief or comfort." This linguistic foundation encapsulates Noah's mission and the divine mandate he received to build the ark, a vessel of salvation amidst the world's impending judgment by floodwaters. Noah's life and the ark he built represent a turning point from judgment to mercy, chaos to order, and curse to blessing, highlighting the transformative power inherent in his name.

63

Noah's story exemplifies obedience, faith, and divine grace. Water consumed the earth, but the ark served as a beacon of hope, a tangible manifestation of God's promise to save Noah, his family, and a remnant of creation, ensuring life's continuation and the possibility of a new beginning. As Noah emerged from the ark onto dry land after the flood, he built an altar to the LORD, embodying the essence of his name by marking a time of rest and renewal for the earth and its inhabitants.

Noah's name has significance beyond the flood narrative. It foreshadows God's restorative plan for humanity, a theme that runs throughout the Scriptures. In a broader theological context, Noah's name and story represent the cycle of judgment and redemption, foreshadowing the ultimate rest and comfort found in Christ Jesus. The New Testament fulfills the Bible's introduction of a new creation by inviting believers into a new covenant of grace, redemption, and eternal rest in Christ.

In essence, Noah's name represents the hope and redemption that come from God's interactions with humanity. It reflects the overarching biblical narrative of creation, failure, redemption, and new creation, encouraging readers to see Noah's story as a foreshadowing of the ultimate comfort and rest that God promises to all who seek refuge in Him. With the cleansing sweep of the flood, Noah ascended to the role of "father of humanity," an echo of Adam's initial mantle.

As the waters receded, a new chapter of creation unfolded, with Noah at its genesis. In a narrative parallel to Adam, who fathered Cain, Abel, and Seth (the bearer of legacy), Noah's lineage through his three sons—Shem (the bearer of legacy), Ham, and Japheth—sprouted into the many nations that populate the world today. Thus, Noah serves as a pivotal figure in humanity's story, acting as a second Adam who repopulated the earth and reshaped history, bridging the antediluvian past with a future filled with endless possibilities and diverse destinies.

The Hebrew term "Noach" (נֹחַ) has a thematic and linguistic connection with the word "nâchâh" (נָחָה), which both convey the idea of rest, highlighting different aspects of how God ushers humanity into tranquility and safety. "Nâchâh" typically represents the act of leading or guiding to a place of rest. This term frequently appears in narratives in which God actively guides His people to a haven of peace, as in Exodus 15:13. The text describes God's merciful leadership, guiding the redeemed to His divine dwelling, a safe haven of rest. "Nâchâh" expresses God's role as a divine shepherd who guides His flock to safety and rest.

In comparison, "noach" refers to the cessation of motion, implying the arrival or existence in a state of rest. Noah is the pivotal figure in humanity's journey to rest. Genesis 8:4, where Noah's ark rests on the mountains of Ararat after the deluge, emphasizes "noach" as a moment of calm and renewal, signaling the end of the flood and a new beginning for humanity and nature.

The biblical narrative's use of "noach" and "nâchâh" suggests an insightful correlation: through Noah, "noach," God effectively "nâchâh" leads humanity to a new domain of rest. Noah's story illustrates the shift from a chaotic world to a restored one, symbolizing the journey from turmoil to peace. Noah's journey, under God's guidance, reflects the larger divine mission of leading creation to ultimate rest and sanctity.

Thus, the nuanced relationship between "noach" and "nâchâh" in Scripture not only emphasizes the themes of guidance and rest but also positions Noah as a conduit through which God restores a world where humanity can find solace and safety. This connection elevates Noah's story from a historical account to a theologically rich depiction of God's relentless pursuit of leading His creation into a permanent state of rest and harmony.

Shem, Son of Noah

The name of Noah's son, Shem, represents deep-seated meaning within the layers of biblical narrative, serving as a foundation for the themes explored in this book. In Hebrew, "Shem" means more than just a

66

name; it also represents reputation, character, honor, and a person's very essence. This nuanced understanding of "name" reflects its critical role in communicating identity and divine inheritance in the Scriptures.

The aftermath of the flood, which tells of divine judgment, deliverance, and the dawn of a new creation, deeply roots Shem's significance. As Noah's eldest son, Shem is at the forefront of carrying on God's covenant with humanity, tracing the lineage that leads to Abraham, Israel, and, ultimately, the Messiah. God's salvific intentions for humanity imprint each name in this lineage, exemplifying the enduring legacy.

Genesis 6:4, which speaks of the Nephilim becoming "men of renown" (shem), intriguingly interweaves the narrative arc surrounding Shem's naming with the larger narrative of Genesis. This reference emphasizes the theme of legacy and reputation, which go beyond individual identity, connecting Shem and his descendants to a divine purpose that shapes the course of human history.

Shem's role and the etymology of his name go beyond familial significance, establishing him as a pivotal figure in the divine-human saga. His name represents the transmission of a godly heritage, identifying his family as bearers of covenant promises and divine favor. Genesis 10's "Table of Nations," which identifies Shem as the progenitor of the Semitic peoples and sets the stage for the fulfillment of God's redemptive plan, further emphasizes this point.

This book, delves into the rich symbolism and theological significance of biblical names, with Shem serving as a prime example of how names function within Scripture—not just as tags but also as carriers of divine narrative and purpose. By using Shem's name, particularly in the context of becoming renowned, the book emphasizes the potent confluence of divine action and human history encapsulated in biblical names.

In doing so, "*The Name Above All Names*" hopes to shed light on the intricate ways in which names in the Bible reveal aspects of God's character, covenantal commitments, and the progression of His salvific plan. Shem's name represents the principle that names in Scripture convey divine and covenantal realities, serves as a lens through which to view the larger story of God's interaction with humanity. It serves as a guidepost for this investigation, emphasizing the transformative power of divine naming in shaping destinies and revealing the ultimate name that encapsulates the essence of God's redeeming mission.

Abram & Sarai

In the biblical narrative, Abram and Sarai emerge as the first people to experience a transformation of identity through God's renaming. Initially bearing names that foretold their individual destinies, they were bestowed with new names by God, signifying a profound redirection in their divine mission. The name Abram means "exalted father," yet with the infusion of the Hebrew letter "Hey" (ה), it was changed to Abraham. However, this modification, contrary to popular belief, does not alter its meaning to "father of many nations" but intriguingly maintains the meaning "exalted father" (Genesis 17:5). This signifies not a change in name or meaning but a pivotal shift in authority.

When you hold authority over something, it is both your right and obligation to name it. Terah, his earthly father, named him Abram, but God renamed him Abraham, representing His divine covenant and promise to him of a legacy far beyond his own family—now he would be the progenitor of many nations. The addition of "Hey" to the name Abram, making it Abraham, signifies God's promise and is akin to Him breathing life into Adam, denoting a renewal, transforming him from merely an exalted father to the exalted father of many.

Abram | Abraham

אברהם | אברם

69

What does it mean for Abraham to be the "father of many nations?" Despite Abraham having eight sons, the translation from Hebrew to English obscures the life-changing truth that Abraham is the father of many "goyim." The Hebrew term goyim, often translated as "nations" or "peoples," means non-Israelite peoples, foreign nations—Gentiles (Genesis 10:5), or all nations including Israel. This understanding carries a much deeper scriptural resonance. Especially when we keep in mind that Abram's transformation into Abraham is a monumental expansion of his role: from the progenitor of a single nation to the spiritual father of all nations, as foretold in Genesis 17:4–5. This transition represents not just an increase in number but also a shift in essence, fulfilling God's promise to bless "all" nations of the earth through Abraham (Genesis 12:3, 18:18, 22:18).

Similar to Adam, Abraham became "the father of humanity," yet his fatherhood transcended biological descent, anchoring instead in a faith that crosses ethnicity and nationality. The Apostle Paul elucidates this paradigm in Romans 4:11–17, portraying Abraham as the universal father of all who believe, regardless of their ethnicity or national identity. This spiritual lineage, based not on the law but on faith, allows everyone to inherit God's promises, making Abraham not only a physical father to his children but also the spiritual father to all humanity.

Paul further reveals that our Lord Jesus Christ heightens this concept of fatherhood, uniting all believers beyond the divisions of ethnicity, nationality, and now even gender. In Christ, all believers become Abraham's seed and heirs of the promise, transcending all earthly divisions to form a singular, faith-bound family (Galatians 3:26–29). This reveals a spiritual kinship that "one-ups" Abraham's role, positioning Christ as the ultimate unifier, where all distinctions and divisions melt away in the embrace of faith.

In this light, Abraham's role as the father of many nations is both a physical reality and a spiritual foreshadowing. His story foreshadows Christ's all-encompassing fatherhood, where faith dissolves all barriers and welcomes everyone into the divine lineage. This thoroughgoing narrative weaves through Scripture, highlighting a legacy of faith that binds all believers across time and space, under the fatherhood of Abraham, and ultimately, in the unity found in Christ Jesus.

Similar to Abram's transformation into Abraham, his wife, Sarai, was also renamed. Sarai's name is derived from the Hebrew word "sar," which means someone of high rank, such as a prince or ruler. It translates to "my princess." With the divine addition of the Hebrew letter "Hey" (ה), her name became Sarah, a name that continues to echo the essence of royalty as "princess" (Genesis 17:15–16). When "Hey" (ה) is used as a suffix it turns a word into a noun. Hence, "my princess" became the proper noun Princess. This simple addition subtly elevated her status from personal to universal, highlighting her new God-breathed role as a matriarch to many nations. Adding "Hey" as a suffix to Sarai's name also suggests a divine blessing of fertility, directly countering her previous struggles with bareness in the promising of the birth of Isaac. This act imbued Sarah with a new identity, divine grace, fertility, and an equally important role in God's Abrahamic covenant.

Sarai | Sarah
שרה | שָׂרִי

God's breath infused the Hebrew letter "Hey" (ה) into Abram and Sarai's names heralding a new chapter of promise and covenant with Him, transforming them into Abraham and Sarah. This act wasn't merely a name change but a divine intervention signifying their transition from personal legacy to progenitors of nations and bearers of a covenant with the Almighty.

This pivotal moment highlights the far-reaching impact of divine grace, marked by the miracle of birth against all odds and the inception of a legacy far surpassing their individual narratives. Through His divine act, God not only reshaped their futures but also emphasized the transformative power of His word, setting the stage for a life and legacy defined by faith, countless descendants, and the miraculous unveiling of God's plan.

Isaac

The name Isaac, derived from the Hebrew yitschâq (יצחק), has layers of symbolic and prophetic meaning, intertwining humor with the fulfillment of a seemingly impossible promise. Isaac's name originated from the term tsâchaq (צחק), which means laughter. His name is distinguished by the prefix yod (י), which translates to "He laughed." This detail beautifully captures Abraham and Sarah's disbelief and joy simultaneously at hearing God's promise of a child despite their old age. Although Sarah often is the first to come to mind when we recall this laughter (Genesis 18:12), it is actually Abraham's laughter (Genesis 17:17) that inspired God to name their son Isaac. Interestingly, the narrative does not explicitly state that Abraham ever shared God's promise with Sarah, implying a divine insight that both would laugh in joyous-disbelief, hence the name "They Laughed."

Delving deeper into the Hebrew letters that make up Isaac's name underscores that there is always much more than meets the eye. Astonishingly, Isaac's name reveals his parents' ages when he was born, encoded within the letters themselves. The letter Tsade (צ) has the numerical value of 90, which is Sarah's exact age. Chet (ח), has a numerical value of 8, indicating new beginnings. And lastly, Qof (ק) has a numerical value of 100, which astoundingly is Abraham's age. This precise numerical alignment within Isaac's name goes beyond being a reminder of his parents' miraculous laughter but also their ages, intertwining their exact reality with the meaning of their son's name and the life they would build together.

Additionally, because Isaac was the first child born into this covenant, he was the first to be circumcised on the eighth day, which adds to the significance of his name by aligning the numerical value of Chet (8) with the very covenantal practice that represents new beginnings and the sign of God's unending promise, directly in between the ages of his mother and father.

This intricate web of meanings, numerical values, and biblical narratives surrounding Isaac's name reveals the profound depth of God's relationship with His faithful servants. Isaac's name encapsulates not only a moment of human skepticism met with divine humor but also the very essence of God's promise, the miraculous nature of Isaac's birth, and the foundational role he plays in the unfolding story of God's people. Isaac, named after his parents' collective laughter but bearing the marks of divine prophecy and covenant, serves as a reminder of the intertwined nature of God's promises, human doubt, joy, and the fulfillment of what appears to be impossible. Isaac, as a result, serves as a perpetual symbol of God's ability to bring life and hope into situations where things seem impossible, embodying the laughter of disbelief transformed into the joy of realization.

Christian thought deeply ingrains the traditional interpretation of Abraham's sacrifice of Isaac in Genesis 22 as a foreshadowing of Christ's sacrifice. Yet we often overlook Isaac's true significance to the biblical narrative. It is the LORD that commands Abraham to offer his son Isaac as a sacrifice, but ironically, it is "the angel of the LORD" that calls out from heaven and stops him at the last moment, not the LORD. Who is "the angel of the LORD?" This narrative serves as a powerful prefiguration of God's willingness to sacrifice His own Son, Jesus Christ, for the salvation of humanity. However, many often view Isaac's sacrifice as the pinnacle of Christ's foreshadowings, disregarding the profound typology present throughout the Bible.

In Galatians 3:16, the Apostle Paul, leveraging his deep Pharisaical scholarship and understanding of Jewish law and tradition, points to an even greater foreshadowing. He argues that the promises made to Abraham and his "seed" were not referring to Isaac or his descendants per se, but to Jesus himself. Paul's insight reveals a deeper layer of interpretation, suggesting that the very name Isaac, which means

75

"he laughs," carries the greater messianic significance. Readers who are unfamiliar with Jewish hermeneutics, such as the PaRDeS method, may find it difficult to understand this interpretation at first.

Paul's argument is that the true fulfillment of God's promise to Abraham comes through Christ, the promised seed, rather than through Isaac. This understanding deepens the typological reading of Genesis, as it suggests that the events and figures of the Old Testament are not just historical accounts but also carry forward-looking significance, pointing to Christ.

Additionally, Paul draws from Psalm 2, specifically verses 4 and 7, to enrich this typology. He identifies an additional layer of meaning associated with the name Isaac in this Psalm's depiction of God's sovereignty and the declaration of the Sonship of the Messiah. In Hebrew, the wordplay between "he laughs" and the name "Isaac" underscores the joy and triumph of God's plan for salvation, a plan that culminates in the coming of Christ.

This interpretation leads the Christian to view the Old Testament as a multifaceted revelation of God's salvific plan, where prophetic significance imbues even the names and narratives, pointing towards Christ. Paul's analysis, therefore, highlights the importance of scholarly prowess (2 Timothy 2:15) and also invites a deeper engagement with the

Scriptures, seeing Christ woven into the fabric of the Old Testament narrative in ways that are both profound and, at times, surprising. (Luke 24:44)

Jacob

In the Bible, name changes often signify a transformative shift in a person's destiny or character, serving as a divine seal on their life's new path. Jacob's encounter at Peniel (Genesis 32:22–32) is a prime example of such a significant change, demonstrating how a new name can represent a profound shift in someone's life path and relationship with the LORD.

At Peniel, Jacob undergoes a significant transformation. The name "Jacob" (יעקב) means "he who supplants" or "heel grabber," reflecting his early life of cunning and ambition, such as obtaining his brother's birthright and his father's blessing through deception. Astonishingly, in ancient Hebrew, the name Jacob is even more amazing because the word עקב aqeb means heel, but by adding the ancient Hebrew pictograph Yod ـﻟ, it makes a hand appear that looks to be reaching out to grab the word heel.

Aqeb (heel) + ancient pictograph of Yod

עקב ـﻟ

77

However, the mysterious and pivotal wrestling match at Peniel marks an unforgettable moment. A night of struggle with a divine figure that leaves Jacob with a physical limp and a new name: "Israel." His new name, means "he who struggles with God," and represents Jacob's direct encounter with the divine face to face as well as his perseverance and spiritual transformation. This renaming represents a transition from Jacob's human-centered cunningness in his early life to a divinely-oriented character that is defined by struggle, endurance, and a direct relationship with God.

Jacob's name change to Israel is more than just a formality; it marks a shift in his essence and destiny. As Israel, his identity is central to the nation of Israel, the people of God. His struggles, symbolized by his new name, reflect not only personal trials but also a nation's collective struggles and unwavering faith in God. His new identity symbolizes a shift toward a more profound spiritual engagement, marked by perseverance, struggle, and transformation in pursuit of God's promises.

Jacob's transformation into Israel exemplifies the life-changing significance of a name change. Such changes are not just superficial or ceremonial but inextricably linked to one's destiny, character, and relationship with the divine. Through Jacob's example, we can see how a name change in the biblical context represents a divine redefinition of an individual's role, essence, and path, indicating a shift from a past of human scheming to a future of divine struggle and engagement.

Joseph

The name Joseph, יוֹסֵף (Yosef), carries deep significance within the biblical narrative, intricately linked with the Hebrew verb יָסַף (yasaph), which means "to add," "to increase," or "to do again." Interestingly, in Genesis 30:23, Joseph's mother, Rachel, makes a play on words, saying, "God hath אָסַף 'âsaph (taken away) my reproach." This connection between אָסַף (asaph), יוֹסֵף (Yosef), and יָסַף (yasaph) is made explicitly clear in verse 24, where upon Joseph's birth, Rachel declares, "The LORD will add to me another son." Her statement not only clarifies the etymology of Joseph's name, but also foreshadows his eventual removal, setting the stage for Joseph's pivotal role in the Israelites' unfolding story.

Joseph's life embodies the concept of addition and increase, not just in terms of numerical growth, but in a broader sense of spiritual and material blessing despite adversity. The story of Joseph, from his sale into Egyptian slavery by the Midianites to his rise to become arguably the most powerful man in Egypt, exemplifies divine favor and multiplication in the face of adversity. This reflects the wider biblical theme of God's providence and redemption, transforming evil into good for the preservation of numerous lives (Genesis 50:20).

Interestingly, a variation of Joseph's name appears only in Psalm 81:5 as יְהוֹסֵף (Yehosef), incorporating the Tetragrammaton (YHWH) into his name, meaning YHWH will add. This fuller form links Joseph's identity directly with the name of God, suggesting a deeper divine purpose and consecration. It elevates Joseph's narrative from a mere personal triumph to a manifestation of God's ongoing work among His people. Such revelations should compel us to study Joseph's entire narrative more diligently.

Joseph's narrative unfolds as an extraordinary precursor to Christ's life, evoking divine themes of love, betrayal, and redemption on a grand scale. Both Joseph's and Jesus' fathers loved them; they both found refuge in Egypt, and they both suffered betrayal for pieces of silver, although the account of Jesus' betrayal one-ups Joseph at the value of 30 pieces, matching the exact number as prophesied in Zechariah 11:12–13. Nonetheless, through false accusations and trials, they both emerged not as victims but as victorious saviors of their people. Joseph's rise from the depths of the pit and dungeon to the heights of Egyptian power to save his people parallels Christ's journey from death to resurrection, embodying a universal salvation narrative for all.

This narrative arc, in which Joseph saves Egypt and his own family from a devastating famine, serves as a powerful foreshadowing of Jesus' mission to save humanity. Joseph represents a shadow of Christ's saving grace, as God strategically positioned him to be a source of life in the midst of death. Joseph's story exemplifies God's masterful orchestration, transforming what was meant for bad into a pivotal means of blessing and preserving the lineage through which our Savior would come.

Joseph spectacularly fulfilled God's promise to Abraham to create a great nation from his descendants. God carried out a vast plan through Joseph, transforming a family of twelve brothers into millions and preparing the way for Christ's birth. Joseph's life serves as a monumental testament to God's unwavering fidelity to His promises, foreshadowing the arrival of Christ, who would bring abundant life (John 10:10). Through Joseph, we see the divine narrative unfold, in which God meticulously prepares the way for the ultimate act of salvation through Jesus Christ.

The name Joseph, in both its simple and fuller forms, thus encapsulates themes of suffering, redemption, and divine orchestration. It underscores God's sovereign use of individual stories to further His greater purpose, foreshadowing Christ's ultimate redemption. Through

Joseph, the Bible illustrates how God adds, increases, and multiplies, transforming personal hardship into a means of deliverance and blessing for many, mirroring the salvific mission of Jesus Christ.

Moses

Moses, the revered author of Genesis and towering figure who bridges the sacred and historical worlds, has one of the most symbolic and etymologically-surrounded names in the Bible. His name, although not mentioned in the book of Genesis' narrative, is central to it. To fully understand Moses' legacy (shem), we must investigate the intricate interplay of meanings associated with his name in Hebrew and Egyptian contexts, each perspective provides a window into his multifaceted identity and profound destiny. This investigation reveals Moses not only as a character in a story, but also as a pivotal bridge between worlds, embodying a name that echoes throughout history, uniting disparate peoples, and echoing divine purposes.

Hebraically, the name Moses (מֹשֶׁה, Moshe) is associated with the narrative of his infancy, specifically his being drawn out of the water by Pharaoh's daughter (Exodus 2:10). This act of salvation from the river is more than just a dramatic rescue; it represents Moses' providential preservation for a divine purpose tied very closely to Noah's narrative. The Hebrew verb מָשָׁה (mashah), meaning "to draw out," encapsulates this

82

pivotal act, enshrining Moses' destiny as a deliverer and leader who drew Israel out of the water. Thus, the name Moses symbolizes his role as the one who would guide Israel from the depths of slavery through the waters of the Red Sea to the promise of liberation and covenant. Astonishingly, Moses name, essence, and destiny coincide. He was drawn out of the water; he himself drew Israel out of the water, and he drew water out of the rock, not just once but twice.

In contrast, an examination of Moses' name through the lens of Egyptian etymology reveals yet another layer of meaning unbeknownst to today's Bible readers. Ancient Egyptians understood the name Moses, or more precisely the consonantal root "MS," as "born of" or "begotten by," due to the absence of explicit vowels in Egyptian hieroglyphs. This interpretation is especially compelling when considering names like "Rameses" Ra-ms-sw (RMS in consonantal form), which translates to "born of Ra" or "Ra has fashioned him," which can be understood as "Son of Ra." The inclusion of "MS" in Egyptian royal names emphasizes the bearer's lineage or divine affiliation, putting them in a context of sovereignty and divinity.

Rameses:

rᶜ: Represents "Ra," the name of the sun god.

ms: Means "to be born" or "to give birth."

sw: A suffix that means "him."

Together implying—Ra gave birth to him or the son of Ra

This dual etymology of Moses' name—Hebrew for "drawn out" connected to Egyptian "meses" meaning "born of" or "begotten by"—not only emphasizes the multifaceted nature of his identity but also his unique role as a cultural bridge. As the "begotten by" or "the son" in Egyptian culture, Moses embodies the complexities of his upbringing in Pharaoh's palace, with a name that reflects status and lineage. Simultaneously, the Hebrew narrative describes him as the one "drawn out," marked by divine intervention and purpose, symbolizing deliverance and covenantal leadership.

The convergence of these two meanings of Moses' name is more than an etymological coincidence; it reflects the paradoxical nature of his life. Moses, raised by Egyptian royalty, stands at the crossroads of history and destiny, inextricably linked to the fate of the Hebrew people, like Noah, Abraham, and Joseph before him. His name, which bears the imprints of both Egyptian and Hebrew cultures, reflects his role as mediator, deliverer, and lawgiver, bridging the gap between slavery and freedom, human origins, and divine calling.

Furthermore, the Egyptian root "MS" in Moses' name, "begotten by" or "son," contributes to the narrative's theological depth. In being

84

called "son" in the Egyptian context, Moses unknowingly foreshadows the greater Son, a motif later fulfilled in Christ, the only begotten Son of God, who frees humanity from the bonds of sin, by freeing the Israelites from Egyptian bondage. This typological connection enriches our understanding of Moses, not only as a historical figure but also as a forerunner to the ultimate deliverer, with his name containing a promise of redemption and restoration.

But that's not all; the ancient Egyptian hieroglyphic element "MS," which means "begotten of," "to be born," or "to give birth," also correlates with the Hebrew name Moses. Moshe has one final letter in Hebrew, "Hey," which corresponds to not one but two Egyptian hieroglyphs for the letter "h": the reed shelter and the twisted flax. Both images resonate deeply with the biblical account of Moses' discovery. Exodus 2:3-5 describes the infant Moses' discovery in a makeshift shelter of bulrushes twisted or woven into an ark among the Nile reeds. This linguistic and symbolic alignment beautifully connects the cultural and historical narrative of Moses' name and his extraordinary discovery.

Moshe:
Hebrew - Mem, Shin, Hey
ms: Means "to be born" or "to give birth."
h: glyphs of the reed shelter and the twisted flax
Together implying—the son born of the reeds

Essentially, the name Moses unites divine providence, cultural identity, and redemptive hope, encompassing both the act of "drawn out" and the status of "begotten by" (son). It captures Moses' dual existence, straddling the worlds of Hebrew slaves and Egyptian royalty, and foreshadows the reconciliatory work of salvation. Through the lens of his name, Moses emerges not only as a figure of the past but also as a timeless symbol of deliverance, bridging the gap between human struggle and divine promise, between the waters of the Nile and the waters of baptism.

The names of key figures—Adam, Eve, Noah, Shem, Abraham, Sarah, Isaac, Jacob, and Joseph—serve as foundational stones in profound patterns, each revealing deep insights into the concept of "shem" and the significance of names within the Hebrew and biblical lens.

These names, rich in meaning and context, are more than just labels; they are divine narratives encapsulated in human language. They provide insights into understanding "names" from a Hebrew and biblical perspective, where a name is more than just an identifier—it's a story, a prophecy, a divine whisper of what has happened and what is to come. Genesis serves as a introduction on the significance of "shem," teaching us that names contain the essence of identity, destiny, and divine interaction, weaving together the overall framework of God's overarching redemptive plan for humanity.

Chapter Four

IN THE NAME

The expression "in the name" is a biblical idiom that refers to acting on someone's authority or representing their essence and will. Idioms play an important role in the Bible, offering expressions with deeper meanings than their literal interpretations. These idiomatic expressions, based on cultural, historical, and religious contexts, convey complex ideas, truths, and emotions succinctly. The heart of this book lies in the Hebrew understanding of a "name," which encompasses one's essence, reputation, character, authority, and very existence. This understanding is critical for comprehending the biblical phrase "in the name."

The Idiom

The idiom "in the name" weaves through the fabric of the Bible, underscoring the profound Hebraic understanding of "shem." To act or speak "in the name" transcends the mere calling of a name; it signifies acting with God's full authority, as though He Himself were acting through the agent. This embodies not only His explicit approval but also a complete alignment with His character, essence, and purpose. Thus, when someone acts "in the name," it is as if He is acting through them, extending His presence and effecting His will in this world. The calling of a "name" in this context is a declaration of unity with His intentions and objectives, deeply rooted in the shared understanding and mutual commitment to fulfill a common purpose.

The Old Testament repeatedly reiterates the pattern of God's "name" as a representation of His very essence. During Moses' encounter with the burning bush, God revealed His "name" as Ehyeh Asher Ehyeh, a profound trifecta: "I AM THAT I AM," "I WILL BE WHAT I WILL BE," or "I AM WHO I WILL BE" (Exodus 3:14). This emphasizes His self-existence, sovereignty, timelessness, and unchanging nature. Knowing God's "name" meant having an intimate relationship with Him, as He told Moses, "I know you by name" (Exodus 33:12).

The prophets also emphasized the importance of God's "name." Isaiah stated that the Messiah's "shem" would be "Wonderful, Counselor, Mighty God, Everlasting Father, Prince of Peace," revealing His divine nature and attributes.

Isaiah 9:6 contains one of the Bible's most misunderstood and highly impactful revelations. Each given name carries a glory that transcends its English translation. Many of us have rightly believed that our heavenly Father has given His unique names to the child born to us, our Lord Jesus Christ, yet without an epistemology. But one way to reconcile this would be to recognize that the Father and Son are "united." Upon closer inspection, shedding light on these names in Hebrew reveals the truth.

Wonderful: The Miraculous Reveal

Searching the Scriptures through the lens of Hebrew reveals divine secrets so great that they evoke awe. Among these hidden gems is a concept so profound that it encapsulates the essence of divine revelation. Consider the wisdom of King Solomon's Proverbs 25:2 (KJV): "It is the glory of God to conceal a thing: but the honour of kings is to search out a matter." This verse is more than just an invitation; it is a clarion call to enter the sacred depths of Scripture, where God's hidden wonders await the diligent seeker.

One such hidden gem, concealed away in the Hebrew language's linguistic entanglements, is the shem "Pala" (פלא), which means "wonderful" or "miracle." This term encapsulates the miraculous nature of the divine, revealing God's extraordinary acts and essence. The birth of this child, which the Scriptures describe as a miracle, is just one example of the divine's glorious workings. The truly inspiring revelation is that the reversal of "Pala" (פלא) reveals "Aleph" (אלף).

91

This revelation is truly breathtaking. As revealed in Chapter 2, Aleph is the name of the first letter of the Hebrew Aleph-bet but it is much more than just a letter. It personifies the concept of a "Master Teacher," a direct representation of our Heavenly Father. This letter is the cornerstone of divine titles and descriptions, such as Elohim and all designations starting with El (אֵל). When Moses inquired about the divine name, he received the profound declaration "Ehyeh Asher Ehyeh" (אהיה אשר אהיה), each word beginning with the enigmatic Aleph, demonstrating its primacy and centrality in conveying the divine essence.

The transformation of "Pala" into Aleph (אלף | פלא) is more than just a linguistic curiosity; it's a glimpse into divine nature. It captures the inherent wonder and miracle of God's presence and action in this world. This discovery underscores the diverse methods by which the divine engages with us, frequently through concealed patterns, chiasmuses, symbols, acrostics, and reversals awaiting the inquisitive soul to uncover.

Aleph | Pala
פלא | אלף

The Aleph is thus more than just the first letter; it is a symbol of divine teaching and guidance, a reminder of the universe's masterful orchestration by an omnipotent creator. This insight broadens our understanding of Scripture, inviting us to engage in a deeper, more intimate dialogue with God. It inspires us to look beyond the surface and discover the layers of meaning that God has woven into the very fabric of language and the words used throughout the biblical narrative.

In this light, "Pala" becomes a testament to the wonderful, miraculous, and divine mystery that has always been present but frequently overlooked. The revelation that "Wonderful" is Aleph flipped serves as a profound reminder of God's infinite wisdom and the boundless scope of His creation. It invites us to marvel at the divine complexities hidden within the Hebrew Aleph-bet, encouraging us to seek, ponder, and enjoy the glorious wonders of God's Word. The child that was born to us was wonderful. He was with us, yet hidden from us at the same time.

Counselor: The Hebrew Depth of Guidance

At first glance, the title "Counselor" may appear simple. However, its Hebrew root, יָעַץ (yâ'ats), reveals richer meanings encompassing advice, guidance, and counsel. It aims to guide us towards a wise course of action or impart upon us the wisdom needed for decision-making. This concept of the Messiah as the ultimate Counselor is echoed in Paul's first epistle to Timothy, where Christ is portrayed as the sole mediator between God and humanity: "For there is one God and one mediator between God and men, the man Christ Jesus." (1 Timothy 2:5)

In Exodus 28 and Leviticus 16, the high priest served as an intermediary, offering sacrifices and rituals to atone for the people's sins, symbolically mediating between the Israelites and God. On Yom Kippur (Day of Atonement), they perform their duties, offering sacrifices for both their own sins and the sins of the people, thereby demonstrating their mediating role. The book of Hebrews emphasizes Jesus' unparalleled role as our High Priest, as described in the verses 2:17, 3:1, 4:14-16, 5:5-6, 6:20, and Chapter 7. He is both fully divine and fully human, capable of sympathizing with our human weaknesses and making a perfect atonement for sin, thereby giving us direct access to the Father's grace and mercy. This portrayal emphasizes Isaiah's revelation of the Messiah's role in providing divine wisdom and guidance, thus bridging the divine and earthly worlds.

The Mighty God: The Peak of Humanity and Divinity.

In Hebrew, the epithet "Mighty God," God is rendered אֵל (El), which combines Aleph and Lamed, symbolizing being yoked with God. This is a breathtaking revelation of ancient wisdom, considering the yoke not just as a wooden harness but also as a symbol of collaboration and guidance. A pair of oxen, harnessed together within a yoke, cultivated the land. This duo included an elder, seasoned ox representing wisdom and strength, as well as a younger, less experienced counterpart. What's the point? The younger ox walks alongside its elder, absorbing knowledge and skill through shared labor. This practice served as a powerful metaphor for the Ancients, who imagined Elohim, the Creator and Judge, as a masterful elder ox. The Ancients saw humanity as an eager apprentice, joined in divine fellowship, and destined to learn and grow under the guidance of the Most High. This fascinating image paints a vivid picture of the divine-human relationship, where the infinite wisdom of God pairs with the flourishing spirit of mankind in a synchronized movement of learning and enlightenment.

In light of this yoking together of God and man, the biblical narrative outlines four stages or levels of man: from Adam, representing man's potential to mirror the divine; to Iysh, a man of God; in contrast with Enosh, denoting weakness or mortality; and culminating in Geber or Gibbor (גבר), the highest stage of man, signifying strength, power, or warrior. Thus, the biblical narrative portrays the child as the pinnacle of humanity, inextricably linked to God. Philippians 2:6–11 beautifully articulates this concept, emphasizing Jesus' humility, obedience, and subsequent exaltation by God while affirming His supreme authority and divine nature.

The Everlasting Father: A Path to the Divine

The title "Everlasting Father," everlasting is derived from the Hebrew עַד (ad), which suggests a sense of permanence and finality. Through the lens of Hebrew, the letters Ayin ⦿ (eye) and Dalet ܕ (door) together form a picture of "seeing the door" or "knowing the way" to the Father. The Messiah's declaration, "I am the door," captures this imagery. (John 10:9), which reads, "I am the way, the truth, and the life; no man cometh unto the Father, but by me." (John 14:6). This language establishes Jesus as the way to the Father and as a witness to Him, similar to the Hebrew term for testimony (עדה êdâh). In doing so, Jesus becomes the Father's living testimony, embodying the eternal path to the divine.

So far, these titles—Wonderful, Counselor, Mighty God, and Everlasting Father—have invited us to a deeper understanding of the Messiah's identity. Each epithet, rooted in the richness of Hebrew language and symbolism, describes different aspects of His divine mission, such as our guide, the embodiment of divine power, and the eternal bridge to the Father. These insights compel us to consider Jesus' multifaceted roles in the grand narrative of redemption, bringing us closer to the heart of the divine mystery. But that is not all...

Prince of Peace, the Harmonizer of Heaven and Earth

In Hebrew, the Prince of Peace is referred to as "Sar-Shalom." In this context, we translate "Sar" as "Prince," like in Sarai (*see Chapter 3*), but it actually means "Ruler," and "Shalom" as "peace." So "Sar-Shalom" refers to a ruler who promotes peace, harmony, and well-being. It represents that the child born to us will bring peace to both individual hearts and the world as a whole. This title emphasizes the Messiah's role as a peacemaker, reconciling humanity with God and establishing spiritual peace through His redemptive work. It also implies His ability to bring peace to nations and establish a reign of justice and righteousness on earth. "Sar-Shalom" encapsulates the Jewish people's hope and expectation for a Messiah who will usher in a period of spiritual and physical peace, fulfilling God's promises of restoration and reconciliation.

Although many of us associate peace with tranquility, tolerance, quiet, or even a greeting, the Hebrew word Shalom contains an even more profound clarity. Then Jesus said, "Think not that I am come to send peace on earth; I came not to send peace, but a sword." (Matthew 10:34) Why would Jesus say that?! To answer this question, we must "experience" the text. Unbeknownst to us, Jesus is contrasting our definition of peace with what Shalom truly is!

In ancient Hebrew, "Shalom" שלום is depicted through four pictographs:

- Shin (שׁ): ᦉ the picture of two front teeth meaning destroy or devour.

- Lamed (ל): ∠ represents a shepherds staff meaning a voice of authority, teachings or instructions.

- Vav (ו): Υ symbolizes a tent peg meaning to bind together

- Mem (ם): ᗰ depicts water meaning chaos, nations, tongues.

When combined, Shalom depicts the total destruction of the voice of authority attached to chaos...

Jesus introduces a profound paradox in this revelation that dramatically changes our understanding of peace: true shalom necessitates the destruction of discord, as symbolized by His wielding of the sword. By accepting His role as the Prince of Peace, as prophesied by Isaiah, Jesus clarifies an important truth. He did not come to offer a false sense of calm, often mistaken for tranquility. His mission is to usher in transcendent peace, which requires the complete eradication of every deceptive voice, doctrine, and decree that arises from turmoil and masquerades as peace. Revelation 20:10–14, where Jesus definitively casts the ultimate symbols of disruption—Satan, Hades, and Death—into the Lake of Fire, reaches the pinnacle of this transformative concept. Through this act, Jesus fulfills the promise of peace by creating a future where true shalom reigns, free of the shadows of pretense.

In My Name

The idiom "in my name" in the New Testament has a strong resonance with the Hebraic concept of "shem," emphasizing a fundamental principle in relation to our Lord Jesus Christ, the ultimate manifestation of God's "name" on earth. Christ came embodying the Father's "shem," proclaiming, "I have come in My Father's name" (John 5:43), and serving as the full manifestation of God's essence, authority, and will.

Jesus empowered His disciples to perform miracles, preach the gospel, and carry out His mission "in His name" (Matthew 18:20; John 14:13–14), which goes beyond mere verbal recognition. It represents divine endorsement and authority. Several passages (Luke 24:47; Acts 2:38; Acts 3:6; Acts 8:12,16; Acts 10:48; Acts 19:5; Colossians 3:17; James 5:14; Revelation 14:1; Revelation 22:4) demonstrate the intention of the actions taken "in the name of Jesus" to honor Him and emphasize His dominion in our lives.

The apostles' understanding of "shem" included the implications for identity and belonging. Peter explained how aligning with Jesus' character, authority, and objectives represented by His "name" leads to salvation (Acts 4:12).

The New Testament encourages believers to venerate, declare, accept, and honor Jesus' "name," incorporating it into their identity, committing to His covenant, and living under His authority. Thus, the phrase "in my name" or "in the name of" emerges not as a simple phrase but as a profound acknowledgement of the Hebrew "shem," encapsulating the character, authority, and intentions of the invoked One, particularly the Lord Jesus Christ, God's "shem" incarnate. To act or speak "in His name" means to accept His identity, join His kingdom, and participate in His salvific work, thereby aligning one's existence with the entirety of His nature and desires.

The idioms "in my name" and "in the name of" weave together ideas and meanings that transcend literal interpretations to express profound truths. These phrases express the authority, origin, or source of an action or proclamation. Luke 24:47 and Acts 2:38, among others, highlight Jesus' power and authority, indicating His central role in salvation and reconciliation. This isn't to simply say or baptize "in the name of Jesus," but to speak or act in His name—authority, character, and essence.

The Acts of the Apostles contain numerous examples of these idioms in action, emphasizing the importance of Jesus' name in gospel proclamation and sacrament administration. From healing the sick (Acts 3:6) to baptizing believers (Acts 2:38, 8:12, 16; 10:48; 19:5) and

100

performing miracles (Acts 3:6), the disciples recognized His sovereignty and authority.

In Colossians 3:17, Paul encourages believers to do everything in the name of Jesus, acknowledging Him as the source of all blessings and gratitude. This idiom emphasizes the deep bond between believers and Christ, acknowledging His authority over all aspects of life.

Called By My Name: Identity and Belonging

The biblical phrase "called by my name" unveils a profound revelation of divine identity, belonging, and covenantal intimacy. It goes beyond simple labels, drawing us into the essence of being known and claimed by God Himself. Isaiah 43:7 brilliantly sheds light on this truth: "Even every one that is called by my name: for I have created him for my glory, I have formed him; yea, I have made him." This verse not only emphasizes the responsibility and privilege of those who bear God's name but also describes a transformative journey of repentance, communion, and restoration. God promises to respond to His people's humble repentance, prayer, and seeking His face (2 Chronicles 7:14), demonstrating His faithful covenant with those who are "called by His name."

This divine invitation reaches across the scriptural landscape, welcoming everyone into a covenant community regardless of nationality or background. James quotes the prophet Amos in Acts 15:17, affirming that this sacred call includes Gentiles, signifying a revolutionary expansion of God's family (Amos 9:11–12). The promise of salvation for all who call on "the Name of the LORD," echoed in Joel 2:32 and repeated in the New Testament (Acts 2:21; Romans 10:13), emphasizes the universality of God's salvific grace and the inclusiveness of His divine invitation.

Isaiah speaks of giving those who follow God's ways "an everlasting name" (Isaiah 56:5), while Revelation 2:17 mentions a new name written on a white stone, symbolizing a unique and eternal legacy for the faithful. This bestowed name goes beyond mere identification, containing the promise of inheritance and an unbreakable bond with the divine.

Exodus 33:12 beautifully captures the intimate dynamics of this relationship as God addresses Moses "by name," demonstrating the depth of familiarity and affection God desires with His chosen ones. To be known "by name" by God is to enter into an extraordinary fellowship with the Creator, characterized by intimacy, trust, and love.

Thus, the idiom "called by my name," is enhanced by the covenantal framework of 2 Chronicles 7:14, crossing linguistic boundaries to reveal the essence of divine calling. By embracing our God-given identity, we acknowledge Christ's sovereignty over our lives and the sublime honor of intimate alignment with God. This call is more than just an invitation; it is a profound recognition of our place in God's grand narrative, a narrative that promises healing, redemption, and a deep enduring connection with the Almighty, highlighted by the grace, mercy, and love inherent in being "called by His name."

Taking the Lord's Name in Vain

God's words, known to us as the Third Commandment, in Exodus 20:7 declares, "Thou shalt not take the name of the LORD thy God in vain; for the LORD will not hold him guiltless that taketh his name in vain," encapsulates ideas based on a deep understanding and reverence for the divine name. This is vital because those of us who take the name of the LORD impact how others perceive Him. When we view this commandment and focus on the Hebrew verb nasa (נשא), which means "to lift" or "carry," while "in vain" implies falsehood, emptiness, or worthlessness, furthering our awareness of the significance of a name, as understood in the Hebraic view of a "shem," particularly God's name, these words encourage believers not only to avoid misusing His name,

103

but they also highlight the importance of correctly bearing His name in our actions and speech.

To "bear," "carry," or "lift up" God's name involves far more than simply avoiding thoughtless or disrespectful utterances. It entails living in a way that reflects God's character and holiness, literally "carrying" His name with respect and dignity in all aspects of life. This means that when we claim to act in God's name or identify as His followers, our actions must reflect the sanctity and ideals that His name implies. Misusing or bearing His name in vain is thus more than just a matter of speech; it is also a failure to connect one's behavior with the weight and power that His name conveys.

This concept strengthens the notion that a name encompasses an individual's essence or reputation, and God's name symbolizes His presence, power, and promises. Thus, bearing God's name is an act of symbolizing God Himself. When a believer invokes God's name for an oath or a vow, they are calling upon His testimony to be a witness to their deeds, emphasizing the gravity and purity of their commitment.

Furthermore, properly bearing God's name demands that our engagement with the world be in a way that honors God. It signifies a resolve to behave justly, love mercy, and walk humbly with God, as stated in Micah 6:8. Each deed performed in God's name must represent His character, whether in justice, kindness, love, or truth.

This perspective alters how we perceive not only the use of God's name but also our actions as bearers of His name. It encourages a life characterized by thoughtful contemplation of God's attributes, reinforcing the profound impact of our verbal and nonverbal reactions in our daily lives. It encourages the believer to ensure that their actions justify, rather than contradict, the honor and purity of the name they bear.

In essence, the words of Exodus 20:7 serves as a compelling reminder of the larger, ethical implications of calling on God's name. It is not simply a restriction on using His name, whether falsely or irreverently, but a charge to embody the very virtues of the God whose name we bear, turning every act and word into a testament to His influence and authority in our lives. It emphasizes a fundamental aspect of Hebraic thought: a person's shem, or in this case, the divine name, is more than just a name; it represents essence, character, and authority. As a result, misusing the divine name is more than just disrespectful speech; it is an affront to God's very nature and relationship with His people.

With this in mind translating Hebrew names into other languages, like נח (Noach) into "Noah," reduces the connection between a name and its bearer's function. Noah's name (נח) translates to "rest" or "comfort," symbolizing his role in bringing humanity a fresh start. Translations can lose the rich web of meanings, associations, and theological implications woven into names when it reduces them to mere identifiers. In English, the linguistic interplay between Noah's name and divine grace is a treasure lost to translation. Interestingly, the Hebrew name for Noah, Noach (נח), mirrors the Hebrew word for grace, chen (חֵן). This amazing reversal connects Noah directly to the concept of grace while also illuminating a much deeper narrative. Noah stood out in the midst of humanity's descent into wickedness, where every inclination of the human heart was inherently evil (Genesis 6:6). His life, symbolized by the continuous Nun נ separating himself from evil, represented by Chet ח, highlights a life in stark contrast to the prevailing moral decay. This divine wordplay reminds us that God found a vessel for His grace in Noah, a beacon of righteousness and hope in a world overcome by darkness.

Noah | Grace

חן | נח

This loss of depth is especially poignant when it comes to the name of God, YHWH. The commandment against taking His name in vain emphasizes the sacredness of God's name, which reflects His unquantifiable essence, covenantal fidelity, and presence among His people. It evokes profound respect and awe, urging believers to recognize the gravity and significance of invoking the divine name. We must approach the name of God with sacred responsibility in all utterances and invocations, reflecting the depth of the relationship and covenantal commitment between God and His people.

Chapter Five

THE NAME JESUS

The Hebrew name "Yeshua," more commonly referred to as Jesus, is extremely important in the context of Judeo-Christian theology and history. At its core, "Yeshua" means "salvation" or "to rescue" in English. Yeshua is the Second Temple Period short form of Yehoshua, which means "YHWH is Salvation" or "YHWH Saves." This name encapsulates the essence of Jewish tradition's messianic hope, which is fulfilled in the person of our Lord Jesus Christ.

The concept of salvation has deep roots in Jewish tradition, and it is intertwined with the story of deliverance and redemption that runs throughout the Bible. Although salvation is often associated with the New Testament, it is also a central concept in the Old Testament. The theme of salvation pervades Jewish scripture, from Exodus, when God rescued the Israelites from slavery in Egypt, to prophetic visions of a future Messiah who would deliver and restore God's chosen people. The name "Yeshua" reflects the desire for divine deliverance and restoration.

In Christian theology, the name Jesus has a unique and profound significance because it refers to our Lord, whom we believe to be the long-awaited Messiah prophesied in the Old Testament. The Gospel's narratives present Jesus of Nazareth as the embodiment of salvation, fulfilling the Jewish people's messianic expectations. According to Matthew, He was to be named JESUS: for he would save his people from their sins. (Matthew 1:21). Through His teachings, miracles, death, and resurrection, Jesus offers redemption and reconciliation with God to all who believe in Him.

The significance of the name "Jesus" extends beyond linguistics to theology. It serves as a reminder of God's faithfulness in keeping His promises of salvation and deliverance. As the incarnate Word of God, Jesus embodies salvation, providing humanity with hope and forgiveness.

Furthermore, the name Jesus emphasizes the close relationship between the Old and New Testaments, bridging theological differences between Judaism and Christianity. We believe that Jesus is the culmination of God's redemptive plan, fulfilling the Old Testament prophecies and promises. By embracing Jesus as "Yeshua"- Savior, Deliverer, and Redeemer- we affirm our faith in the ongoing nature of God's salvific work.

The meaning of "Yeshua" goes beyond its linguistic and theological dimensions and includes the personal aspect of salvation. As we grapple with sin, brokenness, and existential questions, the name

"Jesus" shines as a beacon of hope and salvation. It represents the Father's offer of forgiveness, healing, and restoration to all who believe that He sent His Son to save, deliver, and redeem humanity. It has transformative power, as believers, we encounter the reality of salvation in our lives. Faith in our Lord Jesus Christ reconciles us to God, adopts us into His family, and empowers us to live lives of meaning and significance.

His name, whether spoken in Hebrew "Yeshua", Greek "Iesous", Latin "Iesvs", English "Jesus" or translated into other languages, remains a testament to God's faithfulness, grace, and love for us all.

Yasha

The name Jesus is derived from the Hebrew word "yasha," which means "to save" or "deliver." Exploring the ancient Hebrew pictogram "yasha" provides insights into Jesus' mission and character.

In ancient Hebrew, "yasha" is represented by three pictographs: Yod (י) depicts a man's hand reaching to grasp something ᴗᴵ, conveying the concepts of work, throwing, or worship.

Shin (שׁ) symbolizes two front teeth ᴗᴼ that can bite, consume, or destroy, conveying sharpness or cutting.

Ayin (ע): Represents an eye ⬤, especially one that sees or watches, conveying knowledge or experience.

Combining these pictographs, we decipher that יָשַׁע, or "yasha," translates to "lift up," not to be confused with יִשָּׂא yisa "lift up" as used in the sense of taking the LORD's name in vain. The yod (hand) reaching represents lifting, whereas the shin (teeth) indicates the effort or force used to achieve the lift. The ayin (eye) represents understanding and skill, implying that the act of lifting requires knowledge and proficiency.

This imagery demonstrates that Jesus' mission was calculated and highly strategic. Yeshua, the Savior, is shown reaching down "to lift" humanity from sin's grasp. His humility is inherent in this image, as He humbled Himself to live among us and eventually sacrificed Himself for our salvation. Thus, Yeshua embodies the concept of the Savior reaching down to lift and reconcile us with the Father.

In essence, Yeshua personifies the Savior's role, demonstrating His profound love and sacrificial nature. He descended from heaven to earth, bearing a name that depicts God's salvation and deliverance. By living a perfect life and willingly enduring the cross, Jesus paid the price for our sins, bringing us redemption and reconciliation with God.

Reflecting on the Hebrew name Yeshua reminds us not only of Jesus' saving power, but also of His humility and selflessness. Jesus humbled Himself to lift humanity out of the depths of sin and despair, just as a rescuer would bend to lift another. Thus, Jesus' name is a beacon of hope and a reminder of His unwavering love for humanity.

Deliverance

We continue our exploration of the name Yeshua by delving deeper into the concept of deliverance and its layers, each of which sheds light on Jesus' divine nature as the ultimate deliverer and savior.

Salvation belongeth unto the LORD: thy blessing is upon thy people. Selah. (Psalm 3:8, KJV)

In Psalm 3:8, the Hebrew word "Yeshuah," translated as "salvation," encompasses the concept of deliverance and redemption, illustrating both physical rescue and spiritual renewal. This term captures the essence of comprehensive salvation, highlighting liberation on both physical and spiritual levels.

The proper name "Yeshua," derived from the same root as "Yeshuah," carries a deeper significance as it means "YHWH is salvation." This name underscores the divine nature of salvation,

113

emphasizing that this salvation, deliverance, and redemption come directly from YHWH. "Yeshua" represents the embodiment of God's saving power and His intention to provide complete liberation and renewal to humanity. Thus, the term "Yeshuah" in Psalm 3:8 reflects the act of being saved while also pointing to the profound distinctions of the spiritual and eternal implications tied to the name "Yeshua."

As we journey into the New Testament the concept of deliverance is given even greater clarity. In Luke 4:18, we find the Hebrew word "dror" (דְּרוֹר), translated as "deliverance" or "freedom," which denotes the granting of liberty or release to captives. This passage emphasizes Jesus' mission as Savior to bring freedom and liberation to those bound by sin and oppression, echoing Isaiah's prophetic statement about the Messiah's role in setting the captives free. Jesus made this abundantly clear by reading the scroll of Isaiah (Luke 4:17-21).

Thus, the proper name Yeshua has a wide range of implications, from YHWH physically rescuing to spiritual redemption, while highlighting Jesus' profound impact as the ultimate manifestation of YHWH's deliverance. His ministry exemplifies the fulfillment of these ancient Hebrew concepts by extending God's saving grace to all who believe, granting freedom and liberation from the bonds of sin.

114

The Journey from Yehoshua to Jesus

The transition from the Hebrew shem Yehoshua (Joshua) to the English name Jesus is a fascinating linguistic and historical journey that reveals the complexities of language, transmission, and cultural interaction. This transformation spans centuries and includes changes in alphabets, phonetics, and cultural contexts, ultimately shaping how we address and perceive one of history's most influential figures.

Yehoshua, holds profound significance, meaning "YHWH is Salvation" or simply "YHWH Saves." The Christian Old Testament comes from the Hebrew Bible called the TaNaKh, which is an acronym for T*orah*, N*evi'im* (Prophets), and K*etuvim* (Writings). Yehoshua appears as a prominent figure, known for leading the Israelites after Moses' death and bearing a name laden with divine connotations. However, as cultures intersected and languages intertwined, the journey of this name took unexpected turns.

The Greek Septuagint, the result of 72 Jewish sages translating the Hebrew Scriptures into Greek, marks a pivotable moment in this journey. Certain sounds that were present in Hebrew were absent from Greek, making transliteration difficult. Consequently, the Hebrew "Yeh" (יה) sound transforms into the Greek "Iē" (Iη), while the "sh" (שׁ) sound becomes the Greek "s" (σ). Thus, the Hebrew Yehoshua transforms into the Greek "Iesou".

Forms:

Ἰησοῦς - Ἰησοῦ - Ἰησοῦν
Iēsous - Iesou -Iesoun
Nomative - Dative - Accusative

The linguistic transition from Hebrew to Greek posed unique challenges. Greek male names frequently end in "s," reflecting the language's grammatical conventions for masculine nouns. The Hebrew name Yehoshua (יהושע) was adapted into Greek by modifying the ending to fit gendered naming conventions. The Hebrew name Yehoshua, which ends with the sound represented by the Hebrew letter ayin (ע), was converted into Greek by following the Greek practice of rendering foreign names into a form agreeable to Greek phonetics and grammatical rules. To fit into the Greek naming system, Yehoshua is renamed "Iēsous" (Ἰησοῦς), with the nominative masculine ending "s". This adaptation did more than just add a "s" to match male conventions; it also involved transliterating the entire name into a form that Greek speakers could pronounce and recognize as masculine.

The transition from "Iēsous" to "Jesus" in English highlights the unique evolution of the letters "I" and "J." Originally, these two letters were interchangeable, with "J" appearing as a separate letter much later in the history of the English alphabet. The Greek word "Iēsous" became "Jesus" in English, but the distinct "J" sound was not established until around 1524. This shift highlights language's dynamic and adaptable nature, demonstrating how alphabetic and phonetic changes over time can have a significant impact on name transliteration and pronunciation. While the English name "Jesus" may appear distant from its Hebrew origin, it reflects the complexities of linguistic borrowings and cultural exchanges. The transition from Yehoshua to Jesus goes through Greek, Latin, and English, with each layer adding nuances to the name's evolution.

The Name Jesus in the First Century

History provides an extraordinary glimpse into the various ways people would have referred to Jesus during His lifetime. Contrary to popular belief, during His earthly life, people did not always refer to Jesus by His Hebrew name, Yeshua. In first-century Judea, under Roman rule, "Iēsous" was the Greek pronunciation of Jesus' name, heard in the streets and marketplaces. This glimpse into the past not only demonstrates the rich linguistic and cultural interplay of Jesus' time, but it also dramatically challenges the notion that He was known solely as Yeshua. It showcases the flexibility and adaptability of names in various languages and cultures, illuminating the diverse ways Jesus' name manifested during His time among us.

Pilate's inscription on the cross emphasizes this diversity, with variations of Jesus' name in Greek, Latin, and Hebrew, shedding light on ancient Judea's multilingual environment. Despite linguistic variations, the name's underlying essence remains consistent, representing salvation and divine intervention.

Hebrew - ישוע הנצרי ומלך היהודים

Greek - Ἰησοῦς ὁ Ναζωραῖος ὁ βασιλεὺς τῶν Ἰουδαίων

Latin - IESVS NAZARENVS REX IVDÆORVM

Critically, claims that the name "Jesus" was nonexistent before 1524 due to a lack of a distinct "J" sound overlooks crucial linguistic and historical nuances. The usage of "Iesous" for Yeshua in Greek predates Jesus' manifestation in the flesh by centuries, emphasizing the continuity of meaning across linguistic shifts.

The journey from Yehoshua to Jesus encapsulates the intricate interplay of language, culture, and history. Through translations, transliterations, and cultural adaptations, the name transcends linguistic barriers, embodying the enduring message of salvation and deliverance. Despite linguistic variations, the essence of the name persists, Savior! It serves as a timeless symbol of hope and redemption.

Popularity of the Name Jesus

In the first century, in Judea and Galilee, a variety of Hebrew male names were prevalent, reflecting the diverse cultural and religious landscape of the region. Among the most popular names were Shim'on (Simon), Yosef (Joseph), Yehudah (Judah), Yohanan (John), and Yeshua (Joshua), known to most of us as Jesus. These names were not only common but also carried significant cultural and religious meanings.

We can see how common names were by simply looking at the names of the 12 Apostles:

"And when it was day, he called unto him his disciples: and of them he chose twelve, whom also he named apostles; Simon, (whom he also named Peter,) and Andrew his brother, James and John, Philip and Bartholomew, Matthew and Thomas, James the son of Alphaeus, and Simon called Zelotes, And Judas the brother of James, and Judas Iscariot, which also was the traitor." (Luke 6:13-16, KJV)

Luke reveals that there is a lot of name duplication among the twelve Apostles. Notably, two share the name Simon: Simon Peter and Simon the Canaanite, also known as Zelotes. Similarly, there are two Jameses in the ranks: James, Zebedee's son, and James, Alphaeus' son. To add to the symmetry, there are two Apostles named Judas: James' brother Judas and the infamous Judas Iscariot. Surprisingly, six of the twelve Apostles share their names with one another, leaving only Andrew,

Matthew, John, Philip, Bartholomew, and Thomas with unique names among the selected twelve. This revelation reveals a fascinating pattern in the composition of the Apostolic Assembly.

In the biblical narrative, we see a similar pattern of popularity for the name Mary among various significant women. We begin with Miriam, Moses and Aaron's sister, who played a pivotal role in the Exodus story. Then there's Mary, Jesus' beloved mother, whose place in Christian tradition is unparalleled. Mary Magdalene, a devoted follower of Jesus and witness to the resurrection, further emphasizes the importance of that name. In addition, Martha and Lazarus' sister, Mary, is well-known for her interactions with Jesus. And lastly, Mary, James' mother, joins the list of notable women with this common name, demonstrating the multifaceted and interconnected narratives found in biblical accounts.

In the rich narratives of biblical texts, a fascinating complexity emerges: the name Jesus was not unique to our Lord, Jesus of Nazareth, the Messiah. The New Testament introduces us to several people with this name, including Jesus, also known as Joshua from the Old Testament, Jesus Barabbas, Jesus called Justus, and, of course, Jesus of Nazareth. This intriguing overlap is not purely coincidental; it reflects the popularity of certain names in the Jewish community at the time. Such a revelation highlights the vibrancy and depth of historical and cultural contexts, challenging us to recognize the layers of meaning and identity that names can carry in the biblical era. Far from being a source of confusion, the diversity of Jesuses provides a glimpse into the interconnected world of the Scriptures, where names weave through stories, connecting the past and present in a rich continuum.

Barabbas

Matthew 27:17-18 in the Codex Sinaiticus, the oldest handwritten copy of the New Testament to date:

*"ἦν οὖν αὐτῷ συνήχθησαν ἔλεγεν αὐτοῖς ὁ Πιλᾶτος Τίνα θέλετε ἀπολύσω ὑμῖν, **Ἰησοῦν τὸν Βαραββᾶν** ἢ Ἰησοῦν τὸν λεγόμενον Χριστόν; ᾔδει γὰρ ὅτι δι᾽ ἐνείαν παραδώκεισαν αὐτόν."*

Discovering that Barabbas shared his first name with our Lord Jesus is nothing short of astonishing—a detail that might be entirely new to many. Interestingly, to avoid confusion or misinterpretation, many modern Bible translations have chosen to omit the name "Jesus" from "Jesus Barabbas." This editorial choice, steeped in linguistic and contextual prudence, aims to prevent readers from inadvertently merging the identities of Barabbas with our Lord Jesus Christ. The inclusion of "Jesus" in Barabbas' name could blur the distinct lines between the notorious criminal presented in the Gospels and the sinless savior, Jesus Christ, offered up by Pontius Pilate for potential release. By omitting

121

"Jesus" from Barabbas' name, the translations safeguard the narrative's clarity, ensuring the separation of their identities remains intact and unclouded by potential theological or historical ambiguities.

This revelation that Barabbas also bore the name Jesus enriches the Gospel narrative with profound layers, presenting a captivating dilemma to the audience: were they to choose a "Savior" implicated in sedition and murder (Luke 23:25), or one who, beyond Pilate's declaration of innocence, was the epitome of purity? This compelling contrast not only deepens the narrative's complexity but beckons us to engage more thoughtfully with the themes of innocence, guilt, and redemption that permeate the Gospels, inviting a reflective journey into the essence of salvation itself.

The Other Jesus'

It may come as a surprise to many but there are even more Jesus' in the New Testament. In Acts 7:44–45, reference is made to Moses' Joshua of the Old Testament, who accompanied the Israelites into the possession of the Gentiles. We can easily see that our Lord Jesus is not the only one whose name was transliterated from Greek (Iesous) to English. Nevertheless, Jesus (Moses' Joshua) is not to be confused with our Lord Jesus, but rather reflects the commonality of the name within Jewish history. Similarly, the mention of a Jesus named Justus in

Colossians 4:11 underscores the diversity of individuals with this name in biblical narratives. These instances underscore the need for careful consideration of context and historical background when interpreting biblical texts.

The significance of names extends even beyond mere identification, with many names carrying symbolic and theological meanings. For example, Barabbas, meaning "son of the father," presents another stark contrast to Jesus, the true Son of God, emphasizing themes of substitution and redemption.

Did you know that in the New Testament there is a sorcerer whose father was also named Jesus? It is true! Take a look; it's in the Holy Book! In Acts 13:6–12, we discover a man named "Bar-Jesus," also known as Elymas (Wizard), who opposed Paul's attempts to spread the gospel. Bar-Jesus name is quite significant because it emphasizes the fact that the name "Jesus" was very popular among Jewish people at the time. Despite having the same name as our Lord Jesus Christ, the Son of God, Bar-Jesus the Sorcerer, used his powers to impede the spread of the Gospel. This contrast emphasizes the spiritual conflict between the true power of our Lord Jesus and the deceptive practices of those who oppose Him. Ultimately, when Paul struck him blind, Bar-Jesus encountered the power of the true Jesus, demonstrating the Lord's superiority over all other powers and authorities.

Overall, a deeper look into many of the most popular names in first-century Judea provides insights into the cultural, religious, and linguistic dynamics of the time. Through careful analysis of biblical texts and historical sources, we gain a deeper understanding of the individuals and events shaping ancient Judean society.

Dispelling Myths: The Connection to Zeus

Is there a correlation between the name Jesus and the Greek god Zeus? Absolutely not! One of the greatest misconceptions surrounding the name Jesus is its alleged connection to the Greek god Zeus. Contrary to popular belief, Jesus has no association with Zeus whatsoever. The similarity in pronunciation lies solely in the sigma shared by the names Jesus and Zeus. The journey from Yeshua to Jesus is a testament to linguistic evolution and cultural adaptation, devoid of any mythical connections.

There is a misconception floating around that using the name "Jesus" somehow links the believer to Zeus, or worse, that it's disrespectful to call our Lord anything other than His Hebrew name, Yeshua. It's time to dispel these myths once and for all!

As previously stated, the name "Jesus" actually finds its roots in the Greek "Iēsous," which in turn stems from the Hebrew "Yeshua." There were two variations in Hebrew: Yehoshua and Yeshua. The latter, Yeshua, emerged around 600 BCE as the dominant form during the Roman period.

Throughout history, various pronunciations of "Yeshua" existed, reflecting regional and linguistic differences. Whether it was "Iesous" in Greek, "Iesvs" in Latin, or "Yeshua" in Hebrew, the variations were diverse. The linguistic journey from Hebrew to Greek (Iēsous), then Latin (Iesvs), and finally into English as "Jesus." This evolution had nothing to do with Zeus but rather reflects the linguistic transitions between languages.

While some may draw parallels between "Iesous" and "Zeus," their resemblance is merely stems from the sound of the sigma present in both names.

$$\text{Jesus} = \text{Ἰησοῦς}$$
$$\text{Zeus} = \text{Ζεύς}$$

The single similarity in Ἰησοῦς and Ζεύς is the ς. The sous in Iesous and Zeus only sound similar.

Hebrew = יְשׁוּעַ (Yeshua)

Greek = Ἰησοῦς (Iesous)

Latin = Iesvs

English = Jesus

Let the evidence shatter this myth with undeniable clarity: invoking the name "Jesus" does not, in any sense, diminish our Savior or link Him to Zeus. This notion is purely a product of misunderstanding linguistic evolution, from Hebrew through Greek to English, completely free from any mythological connotations. So, when faced with claims trying to intertwine Jesus with Zeus or demands to exclusively use the Hebrew name Yeshua, stand firm in the true origins of the name "Jesus." Embrace it with full confidence, knowing its transformation across languages underscores its divine uniqueness, not mythical confusion.

Joshua: Precursor to Jesus

Delving into the biblical narrative reveals Joshua as not merely a historical figure but a precursor to Jesus, mirroring Him not only in name but through deep thematic connections. Joshua, initially Moses' aide and later Israel's leader, is a compelling archetype of Jesus, epitomizing spiritual leadership and deliverance. One of the most captivating aspects of Joshua's story is the transformation of his name, which originally was not Joshua but Oshea. Joshua is introduced to us in Numbers 13:8 as

126

Oshea, son of Nun, from the tribe of Ephraim, a significant shift occurs when Moses renames him Jehoshua. The Hebrew linguistic lens magnifies the significance of what at first glance may seem to be a minor renaming.

Oshea, meaning "deliverer," derives from the Hebrew root yasha, embodying the act of salvation. Moses' decision to change Oshea's name to Jehoshua was far from arbitrary; it was a deliberate act to redefine his destiny. By prefacing Oshea with a Yod (י), transforming it into Yehoshua, Moses shifted the meaning to "Yahweh is Salvation" or "Yahweh Saves," highlighting that salvation comes from God, not man. As mentioned in Chapter 2, this subtle yet profound change is the very same careful linguistic choice made when preferring Yehovah over Ehyeh, emphasizing God as the eternal being. Through the simple addition of a Yod (י), Moses redirected the focus from Joshua as the deliverer to God as the ultimate source of salvation, setting a powerful precedent that resonates with the essence of Jesus' mission. This linguistic nuance not only enriches our understanding of Joshua's role but also beautifully prefigures the salvific work of Jesus, affirming God's sovereign role in salvation.

Hoshea הושע

Yehoshua יהושע

To further debunk popular misconceptions, the name Jesus embodies a divine pattern found in the transition of the name from Yehoshua to Yeshua, while preserving its profound meaning, highlights the pivotal truth that salvation is the work of YHWH.

The Scriptures underscore this fundamental principle throughout, as Isaiah's powerful affirmations emphasize:

"I, even I, am the LORD, and apart from me there is no savior." (Isaiah 43:11)

"You will know that I, the LORD, am your Savior and your Redeemer, the mighty One of Jacob." (Isaiah 60:16)

At a glance, these declarations might seem distant from the New Testament's message of salvation. Yet, they find a resounding echo in John 3:16, arguably the most celebrated verse in the Bible, which declares, "For God so loved the world, that he gave his only begotten Son, that whosoever believeth in him should not perish, but have everlasting life."

At the heart of this verse lies a pivotal question: Who does "him" refer to? Jesus or God? A closer look at John 3:16–18 reveals that it is God's unparalleled love that initiates the gift of salvation, through His

Son, to humanity. Often overlooked, Jesus' statement, "Because he hath not believed in the name of the only begotten Son of God," prompts us to reflect on the authority that sent the only begotten Son. This verse underscores that belief in God, the giver of salvation, is the pathway to eternal life, highlighting the significance of acknowledging the authority behind the name of the only begotten Son. While the New Testament vividly presents salvation, Isaiah's declarations that YHWH alone is the savior underscores its deep roots in Old Testament theology.

Yet, this does not in any way diminish Jesus' role in our salvation. His name, Yehoshua, "YHWH saves/delivers," positions Him as the Messiah who manifests YHWH's salvific work. Jesus reveals YHWH's ultimate salvation, fulfilling the prophetic insights of Isaiah (12:2; 43:11; 45:21; 49:26; 60:1, 16; 63:8).

Thus, when we read "For God so loved the world", it is a declaration of YHWH's love, as He offers salvation through His Son, inviting belief in YHWH for eternal life. This narrative, reiterated through Scripture, unveils Yeshua as the Messiah, and the embodiment of YHWH's saving name.

Hebrew Names that Mean Salvation

Elisha - God is Salvation

Hosanna - Save Us Please!

Hoshaiah - YH has Saved!

Hoshea, Hosea, Oshea - Salvation!

Yeshaayahu (Isaiah) - God is Salvation, He is!

Yehoshua, Yeshua, Jeshua, Joshua, Jesus - YHWH is Salvation

A personal pet peeve that surfaces among believers is the frequent use of the expression "my Lord and Savior, Jesus Christ." While deeply rooted in Christian confession and meant to convey reverence, this phrase inadvertently stumbles into redundancy by not fully appreciating the linguistic and theological layers embedded within the names and titles of Jesus. The name "Jesus," derived from the Hebrew "Yeshua," inherently means "Savior" or "YHWH is salvation." Therefore, to say "my Lord and Savior Jesus Christ" essentially doubles down on "savior," echoing "my Lord and Savior Savior Christ."

This redundancy not only reflects a missed opportunity to grasp the rich implications of Jesus' names and titles but also a broader understanding of His multifaceted role in the Christian faith. "Lord," "Savior," and "Christ" are not mere appellatives; they are names loaded with significance. "Lord" acknowledges Jesus' divine authority and sovereignty, emphasizing His lordship over all creation and the believer's life. "Savior" underscores His role in humanity's redemption, highlighting the deliverance He offers from sin and death. "Christ," the Greek equivalent of the Hebrew "Messiah," points to His anointed mission to fulfill God's salvific plan.

Our attachment to the name "Jesus" and His redemptive act of "salvation" reveals a profound truth about ourselves that many of us may have overlooked. Fixating solely on salvation risks overlooking His full identity as Lord, Savior, and Messiah, inadvertently diminishing His sovereignty and overlooking His divine fulfillment of prophecy. Therefore, our devotion must transcend salvation alone, encompassing His lordship and messianic role. Embracing His entirety is essential to truly understanding His divine nature and purpose.

Understanding and distinguishing these names enhances our appreciation of who Jesus is and deepens our relationship with Him. It nudges believers toward a more nuanced expression of faith that not only acknowledges Jesus' identity and mission but also enriches our theological vocabulary and spiritual understanding. Embracing the individual significance of "Lord," "Savior," and "Christ" invites a fuller engagement with the complexity and beauty of Jesus' character and work (shem), fostering a faith that is both informed and transformative.

Given the numerous occurrences of individuals named Jesus throughout the biblical narrative, it is increasingly clear that the name "Jesus" lacks the exclusivity and uniqueness required to be deemed the "name above all names." With figures like Joshua and Jeshua the High Priest, as well as the negative persons of Jesus Barabbas and Bar-Jesus, and others bearing the same name, the sheer prevalence of the name "Jesus" in Scripture suggests widespread use rather than singular significance. While each of these individuals played a role in biblical history, it is our Lord Jesus Christ's life, teachings, and redemptive work that truly elevate Him above all other biblical variations of that name, establishing Him as the ultimate Savior.

Chapter Six

MESSIAH

Within the vast array of Christian vocabulary, one term stands out as universally recognized: Messiah. Commonly equated with "Savior," this understanding, while heartfelt, falls short. As we've seen in the previous chapter the Hebrew name Yeshua directly translates to "Savior." So, what exactly does Messiah mean? In the Hebrew tradition, anointing someone's head with oil was a powerful sacred rite that bestowed authority on kings, priests, and prophets, as well as the title of Messiah, or "Anointed One." Astoundingly, Jesus fulfills all of these roles, embodying the essence of the Messiah, the "Anointed One." Declaring Him as "Lord Jesus Christ" identifies Him as Master, Savior, and King, a magnificent trinity of honor perfectly aligned with His divine purpose.

The concept of the Messiah in Hebrew tradition carries the weight of expectation for a divinely anointed savior who will rejuvenate Israel and usher in a new era of peace and righteousness. This expectation is based on certain messianic qualifiers, particularly lineage. The Gospel of Matthew meticulously maps Jesus' lineage, firmly placing Him within messianic expectations as a descendant of Abraham, David, and, cryptically, Adam. This genealogical documentation is more than just historical; it is a profound theological assertion of Jesus' messianic entitlement, reinforcing His roots as the "Lion of the tribe of Judah"—a powerful symbol of strength, royalty, and divine rule that fulfills the ancient prophecy that the scepter will not leave Judah until the rightful ruler arrives. (Genesis 49:10–12)

The Old Testament describes the anointing of various figures for divine missions, referring to them as "messiahs" in a broader context. Saul and David, as anointed kings, and even Cyrus the Great, whom Isaiah acknowledges as "his anointed" for his edict allowing Jews to return and rebuild the Temple, demonstrate the broad application of anointing.

The New Testament revelation of Jesus as the Messiah connects these Old Testament threads, presenting His life, teachings, and resurrection as the pinnacle of God's salvific plan. This reimagines messianic hopes for a spiritual kingdom beyond earthly boundaries.

Matthew's genealogy does more than just trace Jesus' origins; it declares His identity by anchoring Him in promises made to Abraham, David, and the Messiah, symbolizing His rightful reign. As the Messiah,

Jesus completes the Bible's narrative loop, fulfilling patriarchal promises while embodying God's salvation for all humanity.

Messiahs Throughout Scripture

In ancient Hebrew, oil anointing represented a consecration or setting apart for a specific divine purpose and was frequently associated with positions of significant authority, such as priests, kings, and prophets. This practice elevated the anointed individuals to a sacred status, identifying them as God's chosen instruments for leading, guiding, and mediating on behalf of the people of Israel. According to divine instructions (Exodus 30:22–25), the preparation of the anointing oil symbolized the Holy Spirit's empowerment and sanctification for God's assigned tasks.

The name "Mashiyach" (משיח) does not refer to a single messianic figure in the Hebrew Scriptures, but rather to a group of people who serve as priests, kings, and prophets, each with distinct but interconnected roles within Israel's covenant community.

1. Priests: The priests, particularly the High Priest, acted as go-betweens for God and the people, offering sacrifices and rituals to atone for sins and maintain the covenant relationship with God. Leviticus 4:3 refers to the priest as "the anointed priest" ("ha-kohen ha-mashiyach"),

highlighting his role in atonement and divine forgiveness. The priest's anointing represented his unique consecration to serve directly before God, bearing on the spiritual well-being of the nation.

2. Kings: God established anointed kingship in Israel as a form of divine governance, where the king acted as God's vice-regent on earth, ruling and protecting His people. Prophets anointed Saul, David, and their successors as a sign of their divine selection to lead Israel (for example, 1 Samuel 24:6, in which David refrains from harming "the LORD's anointed"). This anointing bestowed legitimacy and divine authority on the king, tying his reign to the fulfillment of God's covenant promises and justice.

3. Prophets: Although not anointed with oil in the same ceremonial manner as priests and kings, prophets were considered "anointed" in the sense that they were divinely chosen and empowered to proclaim God's word, frequently confronting the people and their leaders with calls to repentance and faithfulness. 1 Chronicles 16:22, "Touch not mine anointed, and do my prophets no harm," emphasizes the prophets' sacred authority as God's spokespeople.

The diversity of anointed roles demonstrates the breadth and depth of the concept of "Mashiyach" in Hebrew thought. It includes not only a future deliverer but also the current reality of God's rule and redemption as mediated by His chosen servants. Each anointed role—priest, king, and prophet—reflects aspects of God's interaction with His people: the priestly role focuses on reconciliation and atonement, the kingly role on justice and governance, and the prophetic role on revelation and guidance.

In preparation for a future Messiah, these three offices converge, pointing to a person who perfectly embodies the priestly ministry of atonement, the kingly rule of justice and peace, and the prophetic declaration of God's word. The New Testament portrays Jesus as the Messiah, uniquely anointed by the Holy Spirit, who establishes God's kingdom, performs the ultimate act of atonement, and fulfills the prophetic word, thereby fulfilling this expectation. Understanding "Mashiyach" in its original context enriches the biblical narrative by revealing the many ways God worked through His anointed servants to reveal His purposes and extend His salvation. It also deepens our understanding of Jesus' messianic identity, linking His mission to the historical and spiritual legacy of Israel's anointed ones and affirming His role as the fulfillment of God's redemptive plan.

Touch Not My Messiah

The Christian appropriation of expressions like "touch not my anointed" ignores the rich Hebraic tradition behind the term "anointed," or "Messiah" (Mashiyach). In the Hebrew Scriptures, the term "anointed" designates individuals, including kings, priests, and prophets, who underwent the ritual of oil anointing to consecrate themselves for God's service. This act symbolized divine selection and empowerment for specific roles in the Israeli community. God originally used the phrase "touch not my anointed" (1 Chronicles 16:22, Psalm 105:15) to emphasize these individuals' sacrosanct status, providing divine protection for their vital roles in upholding His covenant with His people.

In contrast, modern Christian usage of this phrase frequently abstracts it from its original context, implying a broad protection for believers, particularly leaders, without regard for the specific covenantal and communal roles envisaged in the Hebrew concept of "Messiah." This shift not only takes away from the deep, covenantal nuances of being God's anointed, but it also risks misinterpreting the nature of protection and authority it represents.

Furthermore, equating "anointed" solely with spiritual or pastoral leadership while ignoring the comprehensive messianic expectation woven throughout the Hebrew Scriptures can dampen anticipation and recognition of Jesus as the Messiah. He is the one who embodies the fullness of God's promises by combining the roles of priest, prophet, and king in a way that goes beyond and fulfills the ancient expectations of God's anointed ones.

This nuanced understanding of "anointed" as Messiah encourages us to delve deeper into our faith's Jewish roots, recognizing the continuity and fulfillment of the Hebrew Scriptures in the person and work of our Lord Jesus Christ. It encourages believers to reconsider the use of terms like "anointed" in light of their rich theological heritage, fostering a more informed and respectful conversation about the original meanings and implications of these biblical concepts.

King and Messiah

In both Biblical implication and Hebraic contexts, the term "Messiah" (Hebrew: מָשִׁיחַ, Mashiyach) has deep-rooted connotations of kingship, intertwining the roles of king and messiah into a singular expectation of leadership under God's sovereign will. In Jewish tradition, this anointing represented God's selection of the individual to fulfill a specific role within the Israeli community, which was frequently associated with leadership, guidance, and deliverance.

Expectations surrounding King David's lineage establish the strongest association between the Messiah and kingship. The covenant with David, described in 2 Samuel 7:12–16, promises an everlasting dynasty, with a king from David's line establishing an eternal kingdom. This covenant established the messianic vision of a future king who would restore Israel, bring peace and justice, and reign with righteousness. The prophetic books, particularly Isaiah, Jeremiah, and Ezekiel, expand on this theme by revealing the Messiah as a descendant of David who embodies the ideal of divine kingship.

The convergence of the roles of king and messiah in Jewish thought is thus more than just symbolic; it encapsulates the expectation of divine rule through a human agent selected by God. This anticipated figure is both a political and spiritual leader, and His reign will see God's promises to Israel and the nations fulfilled. In this context, the Messiah's kingship is central to His messianic identity, emphasizing His place in God's redemptive plan for the world.

Within Christianity, Jesus is believed to be the long-awaited Messiah. Although conversely, many Jews reject this and are still awaiting the Messiah. The New Testament portrays Jesus as the fulfillment of these ancient promises, tracing his lineage back to David himself (as seen in Matthew 1:1–16). The biblical and Hebrew understanding of the Messiah aligns with this portrayal. However, when considering the broader biblical context, it becomes clear that the name "Messiah" cannot claim exclusive significance. Messiah has also been used to refer to notable figures such as Saul, David, and Cyrus the Great, as well as any of "God's anointed ones." Thus, while Jesus undoubtedly embodies the essence of the messianic role, the mere presence of other significant figures bearing this name reduces the likelihood that "Messiah" is the "name above all names."

Chapter Seven

THE SON OF MAN

The Hebraic concept of "the Son of Man" unfolds as a profound emblem within Scripture, especially when set against the name "Son of God." Traditionally, people view Jesus' designation as the "Son of God" as a declaration of His divinity, while His preference for the term "Son of Man" suggests His humanity. Yet, delving into the Hebrew Bible and New Testament uncovers a fascinating twist to these interpretations.

In the Hebrew Scriptures, "son of God" frequently indicates a special bond between God and individuals, or even the nation of Israel. The Psalms herald the Davidic king as God's son (Psalm 2:7), and this extends to Solomon, who is figuratively considered God's son (2 Samuel 7:14). The term even encompasses Israel as God's firstborn (Exodus 4:22) and Adam as God's son in Luke's genealogy (Luke 3:38), highlighting a designation of divine favor rather than literal divinity.

Conversely, "Son of Man" in the Book of Daniel, particularly in its Aramaic context, takes on another dimension. Daniel's vision of "one like a son of man" granting dominion and glory (Daniel 7) elevates the

143

term to signify a divine or celestial role, diverging from its otherwise human connotation in texts like Ezekiel. Jesus' embrace of this title, especially in foretelling His trials and triumph (Mark 14:62), positions Him alongside Daniel's celestial figure, challenging Jewish expectations and sparking claims of blasphemy.

These linguistic and cultural insights cast Jesus' dual titles in a new light. Far from a mere admission of humanity, "Son of Man" on Jesus' lips claims a pivotal divine role, uniting divinity with humanity. It underscores His authority in God's judgment and His central role as the bridge between God and man, achieving the messianic prophecies of the Hebrew Scriptures and reshaping them through His earthly journey and resurrection.

Acts 2:38 and Acts 9:19–22 depict the early Christian rites of baptism and confession, which echo this nuanced understanding. Here, the early believers' baptism "in the name of Jesus Christ" for sin remission and their acknowledgment of Jesus as the awaited Messiah highlight a deep recognition of His singular role as both Messiah and divine "Son of Man," the gateway to salvation and eternal life.

Therefore, the titles "Son of God" and "Son of Man" go beyond simple descriptions of Jesus' character; they intricately weave into the biblical narrative, unveiling His pivotal role in God's redemptive history.

They encapsulate the mystery of the Incarnation—God becoming man to mend a fractured world—beckoning believers to ponder deeply about Jesus' life and mission. This exploration into "the Son of Man" not only elevates our understanding of Jesus' divine mission but also celebrates the Bible's cohesive and profound narrative, affirming Jesus as the fulfillment of ancient prophecies and the herald of a new covenant, inviting all to become children of God in this grand story.

The Name Jesus' Called Himself

Jesus referred to Himself as the "Son of Man" more often than any other name in the New Testament. This title is used by Jesus approximately 80 times across the four Gospels. Jesus' self-designation highlights His role in fulfilling the prophecies of Daniel 7, emphasizing His messianic mission, suffering, death, resurrection, and ultimate return to glory.

Daniel's vision is absolutely remarkable and unparalleled in all of Scripture. The revelation of "One like the Son of Man," arriving with the celestial majesty of heaven's clouds, is awe-inspiring just as it is. But, unknown to the English reader, this passage deviates from biblical norms by using Aramaic instead of Hebrew. In Hebrew, the "son of man" would be referred to as "ben adam," but Daniel's narrative introduces us to the Aramaic "bar enosh," which is used exclusively in this context throughout the Bible. It is the name "bar enosh" that Jesus chose to identify Himself, intentionally embracing the very unique identity of Daniel's "One like the Son of Man," who was prophesied to arrive with divine authority amidst the clouds of heaven. This distinct self-identification by Jesus not only emphasizes His profound connection to the prophetic vision but also lays the groundwork for His extraordinary role as the one who connects heaven and earth.

In the following chapter, you will discover that unlike "the Son of Man," Jesus rarely referred to Himself directly as the "Son of God"; instead, others ascribed this title to Him, such as Peter's confession in Matthew 16:16, demons recognizing His divine authority (Mark 3:11), and the centurion at the crucifixion (Matthew 27:54). When Jesus speaks in terms related to His divine sonship, He often does so in a more indirect manner, such as in John 10:36, where He asks, "Say ye of him, whom the Father hath sanctified, and sent into the world, Thou blasphemest; because I said, I am the Son of God?" Jesus doesn't directly apply the title to Himself, yet at the same time He does not reject it.

The disparity in the frequency of these titles highlights different aspects of Jesus' identity and mission. The "Son of Man" emphasizes His fulfillment of Old Testament prophecies, His identification with humanity, and His salvific role. The "Son of God" underscores His divine nature and the unique relationship with the Father, affirming His deity and role in the Godhead. Together, these titles encapsulate the mystery of the Incarnation, portraying Jesus as both fully divine and fully human.

Son of Man and the Last Adam

Son of Man and Last Adam are likely two names that many would have never even considered to have any correlation. But through the lens of Hebrew Son of Adam and Last Adam scream, "Look at me!" These biblical concepts serve as profound connections within the tapestry of Scripture, revealing the multifaceted role of Jesus Christ in redemption and restoration. While these names emerge from different textual traditions within the Bible, they converge in their depiction of Jesus as both the fulfillment of humanity's destiny and the inaugurator of a new creation.

The title "Son of Man" is primarily drawn from Daniel 7:13–14 and extensively used by Jesus in the Gospels, particularly in the synoptic Gospels (Matthew, Mark, and Luke). It emphasizes Jesus' humanity, His messianic identity, and His eschatological role in judgment and the establishment of God's kingdom. This portrayal depicts the "Son of Man" as possessing a divine mandate, ascending with the clouds of heaven, and receiving dominion, glory, and an eternal kingdom. This name underscores Jesus' solidarity with humanity, His role as the representative

147

of humankind, and His authority to execute divine judgment and salvation.

The term "Last Adam" appears in 1 Corinthians 15:45, where Paul contrasts Adam, the first man, whose progeny brought death into the world through sin, with Jesus, whom he calls the "Last Adam," who brings life and immortality to light through the Gospel. This name highlights Jesus as the initiator of a new creation, undoing the effects of sin and restoring humanity's intended relationship with God. Jesus becomes the firstfruits of a new humanity through His resurrection, offering eternal life to all who unite with Him in faith. The "Last Adam" thus signifies the completion and transcendence of Adam's role, ushering in a new era of righteousness and life for God's people.

The correlation between the "Son of Man" and the "Last Adam" lies in their shared emphasis on Jesus' unique role in God's redemptive plan.

Both titles illuminate aspects of Jesus' work:

1. Representing Humanity: As the "Son of Man," Jesus identifies with the human condition, experiencing temptation, suffering, and death. As the "Last Adam," He represents humanity in overcoming sin and death, offering the possibility of new life.

2. Inaugurating a New Creation: While the "Last Adam" symbolizes the start of a new creation free from the curse of sin, the "Son of Man" is central to the establishment of God's eternal kingdom.

3. Fulfilling Eschatological Hope: Both titles convey Jesus' role in fulfilling the eschatological (end-times) hopes of Israel and humanity. He inaugurates God's kingdom on earth and secures the promise of resurrection and eternal life.

In essence, while "Son of Man" and "Last Adam" emerge from different scriptural backgrounds, together they paint a comprehensive picture of Jesus' mission. They affirm His connection to humanity, His role as the definitive revelation of God's love and justice, and His victory over sin and death, offering redemption and the hope of resurrection to all who believe. Scripture reveals the depth and breadth of Jesus' identity as both fully human and fully divine, the one who makes all things new, through these names.

The Last Adam

The names Abraham, David, and the Messiah conceal an extraordinary pattern when we explore Matthew's genealogy of Jesus. The first letters of each name, respectively, are Alef, Dalet, and Mem (אדם), which form "Adam." This stunning discovery reveals humanity's beginnings with Adam and our ultimate renewal in Jesus, the "Last Adam." This sequence not only represents a journey from death to eternal life, but it also reflects the Apostle Paul's theological vision of the transition from the earthly Adam to the heavenly Adam.

*"The book of the generation of Jesus Christ (**M**essiah), the son of **D**avid, the son of **A**braham." (Matthew 1:1, KJV)*

The declaration of the Last Adam as heavenly reveals a profound theological truth: Jesus is the personification of divine intelligence, bridging the gap between God and humanity through enlightenment and unity. This theme honors God's intricate plan, weaving a masterful narrative of redemption and hope through the complexities and unpredictability of human history.

This discovery not only reveals the meticulous design of Scripture, but it also emphasizes the seamless narrative that connects the Old and New Testaments, fusing our human experience with divine purpose. Paul's portrayal of Jesus as the Last Adam reveals insights into the depth of God's redemptive plan, encouraging every believer to investigate the Scripture's layered meanings and divine intentions, all while affirming God's promise that all things do indeed work together for the good of those who love Him, according to His purpose (Romans 8:28).

In examining the significance of the name "Son of Man," we come across a profound paradox. While Jesus frequently used this Aramaic expression to distinguish His divine identity from mere mortals, it also serves as a reminder of His human nature. His choice of language, Aramaic over Hebrew, emphasizes His unique position among the sons of men throughout Scripture. However, this distinction reveals an important truth: the name "Son of Man" cannot stand alone as the ultimate "name above all names." Rather, it testifies to Jesus' dual nature—fully human and fully divine—while emphasizing His unparalleled role in redemption. Thus, while "Son of Man" captures the mystery of Christ's incarnation, it does not claim exclusive supremacy, leaving room for the revelation of a higher, more transcendent Name.

Chapter Eight

THE SON OF GOD

O ut of the many names and divine titles revealed throughout the Bible, the name "The Son of God" emerges with a profound exclusivity and significance that transcends the familiar boundaries of names we have encountered thus far. In this chapter, we will elucidate the unparalleled stature of the name "Son of God," a shem that denotes a divine lineage and authority far surpassing any earthly or celestial name, including that of "Jesus" or "Son of Man."

In the Beginning

Opening the Bible to its very first verse, "In the beginning, God created the heaven and the earth," introduces us to a narrative that transcends its simple English translation. The Hebrew word בראשית "Bereshit," pronounced "beh-ray-SHEET," begins Genesis 1:1, carrying a wealth of meaning far beyond "beginning." At the heart of "Bereshit" are the first two letters of the Bible, "Bet" and "Resh," which together spell "Bar," a Hebrew word meaning "son." This foundational coupling of letters invites a rich layer of interpretation right from the outset.

"Bereshit" is associated with "Rosh," a term that signifies "head," leadership, prominence, and origin. When combined with "Bet," which not only means "in" but also visually resembles the layout of a house, the word "Bereshit" frames creation itself as an intimate, familial act. Thus, Genesis 1:1 could be seen as expressing "Through the principal or head, God created the heavens and the earth." This nuanced reading brings forth the image of creation not merely as a demonstration of power but as a deeply relational act, with creation envisioned as a household overseen by a supreme "Head."

The presence of "Bar" within the first two letters of the Bible enriches this interpretation further, embedding the concept of sonship at the very foundation of the biblical text. This intertwines the act of creation with themes of lineage and relationship right from the start, suggesting a divine narrative that is as much about establishing a familial bond as it is about forming the physical world.

The Exclusivity of Son of God

In the depths of ancient Hebrew thought, the concept of sonship is incredibly rich, encompassing not just biological descent but an intricate blend of inheritance, legal and social standing, covenant relationships, and spiritual lineage. This complex backdrop illuminates the extraordinary nature of being called the "Son of God." Far from mere earthly father-son ties, this divine sonship unveils a profound, covenantal connection with the Creator, endowing the anointed with unparalleled authority and mission.

Nicodemus' visit by night with Jesus is a significant moment, subtly intertwining Jewish Messianic expectations with the divine revelation of Jesus' identity. His recognition of Jesus as a teacher who came from God fits into the anticipated Messiah's narrative, but the role of Jesus quickly expands beyond his statement. This interaction ushers in a theological journey from the awaited Messiah to the enigmatic Son of Man, culminating in Jesus' revelation as the Son of God. This evolution both challenges and deepens our understanding of Jesus' purpose, which extends beyond earthly restoration to universal salvation. Through this progression, Jesus fulfills and surpasses messianic prophecies, enacting God's ultimate plan for human redemption. The narrative invites us to explore the depths of God's love and the transformative power of Jesus' mission, from "Messiah" to the "Son of Man" to the "Son of God," which provides a path to eternal life.

This name, "Son of God," carries immense theological depth within Christianity, highlighting a singular identity pivotal for grasping Jesus' essence and mission. More than a term of honor, it demarcates

Jesus' divine stature, setting Him apart from all creation and underscoring the sole path to salvation through Him.

At its heart, the exclusivity of "Son of God" delineates Jesus from other figures labeled "sons of God" in Scripture, such as angels or devout followers. In the biblical vernacular, while "sons of God" may denote beings crafted by God and in communion with Him, the title "Son of God," ascribed to Jesus, intimates a shared divine essence with the Father, beyond mere creation or adoption.

Notably, the New Testament crystallizes Jesus' divine sonship, particularly in John's Gospel, where Jesus, the Logos, coexists with God, manifesting preexistence and divinity. This narrative crescendos in the declaration of Jesus as the "only begotten Son," embodying an unparalleled relationship with the Father, unlike any created being.

Furthermore, Jesus' baptism and the Transfiguration scenes amplify His divine sonship, with the heavens affirming Him as the beloved Son, the chosen vessel of divine will and authority, outshining prior prophets.

This unique sonship of Jesus, central to Christian salvation doctrine, posits that redemption flows exclusively through Him, reflecting

156

His innate unity with the Father. This doctrine is not just an ontological statement but forms the basis for reconciling humanity with God.

In essence, the name "Son of God" for Jesus is foundational to the Christian faith, encapsulating Trinity doctrine, Christ's dual nature, and His exclusive role in salvation. It underscores the profound mystery and grace of the gospel: God incarnate in Jesus Christ, the Son of God, to redeem and reconcile the world.

Biblical Usage of "Son of God"

The appellation "Son of God" in Scripture spans various contexts to denote different divine relationships, yet its application to our Lord Jesus Christ stands unparalleled in significance. Direct affirmations of Jesus as the "Son of God" amplify this distinction, as does the unique context of its usage compared to other scriptural instances.

Adam, termed the "son of God" in Luke's genealogy, highlights his direct creation by God in His image and likeness, yet lacks the divine essence and redemptive purpose intrinsic to Jesus' sonship.

Angels, referred to as "sons of God" in the Old Testament, denote their heavenly origin and messenger roles, distinctly separate from Jesus' inherent divinity and eternal fellowship with the Father.

Israel and its kings, metaphorically called "sons of God," signify a covenantal, chosen status, diverging sharply from Jesus' sonship that embodies divine nature and the fulfillment of God's salvific plan.

In contrast, the acknowledgement of Jesus Christ as the "Son of God" affirmatively proclaims His divine nature, eternal generation, and centrality in salvation. This name, thus, signifies not just a special relationship but an essential oneness with God, distinguishing Jesus from all other scriptural "sons of God."

Christ's salvific work metaphorically adopts Christians as "sons of God," reflecting a transformative relationship. However, this spiritual sonship, while profound, does not equate to the ontological sonship of Jesus but highlights the believers' inclusion in God's kingdom through unity with Christ.

The Only Begotten Son

The theological richness of Jesus as the "only begotten" and the "Son of God" deepens when we explore the biblical significance of "firstborn" within the Hebrew tradition. Here, "firstborn" (bēkōr) implies not merely the first child born but a position of preeminence, honor, and the primary heir. This concept elevates the "firstborn" to a status of distinction, irrespective of birth order, as seen through various biblical narratives where the "firstborn" holds a special place in God's salvific history.

Jesus, being hailed as the "firstborn," transcends the conventional understanding of the term, embodying supremacy over all creation (Colossians 1:15). This title, prophetically linked to the Messiah in Psalm 89:27, indicates a sovereignty and majesty unmatched, prefiguring Jesus' role as the divine sovereign, the pinnacle of God's redemptive plan. His designation as "firstborn from the dead" (Colossians 1:18) further cements His central role in the Christian faith, highlighting His victory over death and His authority as the head of the church.

The title "only begotten" further emphasizes Jesus' unique status. The New Testament uses this term to describe Jesus, emphasizing His unique relationship with the Father and His unique status as the Son of God. Unlike any other being, Jesus shares the same divine essence with the Father, making Him the sole mediator between God and humanity (1 Timothy 2:5).

When Jesus describes Himself as "the Alpha and the Omega" (Revelation 22:13), or in Hebraic terms, the Aleph and the Tav, He is not just declaring His eternal existence but is intricately linking Himself to the entirety of God's Word and plan, from creation to completion. This assertion of being the "First and the Last" mirrors the declarations made about YHWH in Isaiah 41:4, 44:6, 48:12, seamlessly blending Jesus' identity with the eternal God of Israel, further solidifying His divine sonship and messianic role.

The exclusivity of Jesus as the "Son of God" is not just a testament to His divine essence but is integral to understanding the pathway to salvation. It affirms that through Jesus alone—God incarnate, the Word made flesh—can humanity find redemption and restoration. This profound truth is at the heart of Christian faith, encapsulating the mystery of the Incarnation and the breadth of God's love, offering salvation to all through His "only begotten Son." (John 3:16)

Thus, the biblical portrayal of Jesus as both the "only begotten" and the "Son of God" unveils a multifaceted revelation of God's nature and His plan for humanity. It encourages believers to explore the depths of Christ's mystery, fostering a faith that acknowledges Jesus as the pinnacle of God's love and the key to restoring our relationship with the Creator. Through Jesus, the narrative arc of Scripture finds its fulfillment, revealing the depth of God's commitment to redeem the world and inviting all to partake in the divine heritage as children of God through faith in the Son.

The Name Known to Devils

In the spiritual narrative of our Lord Jesus Christ's ministry, a profound recognition of His divine identity is made evident, not just among those seeking redemption but significantly by the forces of darkness themselves. This acknowledgement, particularly the title "Son of God," offers profound insight into the spiritual awareness and acknowledgment of Jesus' divine authority and mission by demonic forces. Through several biblical passages, this acknowledgment unfolds in a series of encounters between Jesus and demonic entities, revealing a complex recognition and response to His divine sonship.

Immediately after the voice from heaven proclaimed, "This is my beloved Son, in whom I am well pleased" (Matthew 3:17), the Temptation in the Wilderness (Matthew 4:1–11) picks right up on the proclamation and serves as an illuminating prelude, where Satan himself challenges Jesus, prefacing each of his temptations with "If thou be the Son of God." This challenge is twofold: it not only questions Jesus' identity but also attempts to provoke Him into demonstrating His divinity independently of God's will. The devil's approach evolves from targeting Jesus' physical needs to questioning His trust in God's protection and, finally, to offering Him all worldly kingdoms in exchange for worship. These temptations reveal a strategic attempt to undermine Jesus' mission by questioning His reliance on and allegiance to His Father, acknowledging His identity as the "Son of God," but attempting to corrupt its purpose.

Further encounters with demonic forces underscore this recognition. In Mark 3:11–12 and Luke 4:41, unclean spirits, upon seeing Jesus, fall before Him, declaring Him as the "Son of God. While these declarations affirm His divine identity, Jesus responds with a command for silence, indicating a strategic restraint in the revelation of His identity at that point in His ministry and also suggesting that the revelation of who He is must come from God alone. Jesus' encounter in the Gadarenes with the Legion (Mark 5:7–13; Luke 8:28) further illustrates this recognition, as those devils not only acknowledge Jesus as the "Son of the Most High God" but also exhibit fear of His authoritative power over them and His ability to torment them, an authority inherent only in His divine sonship.

These acknowledgments by demonic forces have multiple theological implications. First, they affirm the spiritual realm's awareness of Jesus' divine identity and authority as "The Son of God," contrasting the often oblivious or confused recognition by humans. Second, they highlight the kingdom of darkness' understanding of the cosmic battle between good and evil, recognizing Jesus as the pivotal figure in God's redemptive plan. The Legions' reactions—fear, submission, and attempts to negotiate—reflect an acknowledgment of Jesus' sovereignty and the threat His ministry posed to their dominion.

The narrative of these encounters is not merely about the acknowledgment of Jesus' identity by the forces of darkness but also about the authority and mission of Jesus as the "Son of God." Jesus strategically controls the revelation of His identity by commanding silence from the devils, thereby understanding His messianic role through His teachings and miracles, and the Spirit, not through the demons' testimony.

This approach underscores a deliberate unfolding of His identity and mission, aligning with God's redemptive timeline and preserving the purity of the messianic revelation. This deliberate unfolding is made explicitly clear in Matthew 16, where Jesus began by asking, "Whom do men say that I the Son of Man, am? And they said, Some say you are John the Baptist, some say Elias, and others, Jeremias, or one of the prophets." (Matthew 16:13b-14, KJV). But, have we stopped to consider why specifically John, Elijah, and Jeremiah? Exploring the meanings of each one of these name reveals a deep connection to Jesus' identity and mission.

First, consider John. In Hebrew, "Yôchânân" comes from "Yehôchânân," which means "Yahweh is gracious." However, when we recall the story of Noah, we see God's favor manifested in the form of his protection from the destruction of the flood. Thus, the name John more accurately means "YHWH's protection," which not so coincidentally is demonstrated through baptism (complete immersion in water) for the cleansing (remission) or forgiveness of sin, akin to the flood waters that completely immersed the world for the cleansing of sin.

Next, Elijah, or 'êlîyâh in Hebrew, means "My God is Yah." Jesus makes another connection by identifying John the Baptist as Elijah's fulfillment, highlighting their shared missions and message of repentance and return to Yah.

Lastly, Jeremiah, or "Yirmeyahu," translates to "Yah Raised Up." This echoes the promise in Deuteronomy 18:18 of a Prophet raised from among the brethren to speak God's words. Jeremiah's prophecies about the Messiah and God's kingdom are fulfilled through our Lord Jesus, who was eventually raised through resurrection and ascension. But, despite being called these names, Jesus questions His disciples, "But whom do say ye that I am?" Where Peter confesses, "Thou art the Christ, the Son of the living God." To which Jesus responds, "Blessed art thou, Simon Barjona; for flesh and blood hath not revealed it unto thee, but my Father which is in heaven."

It is critical to consider Jesus' renaming of Simon to Peter in Mark 3:16, meaning "rock," in John 1:42, he is given the name Cephas, which is a transliteration of "Kepha" in Aramaic. Four Hebrew letters כאפא make up the name "Kepha," which carries significant symbolism. The letter "Kuf" represents a palm �, indicating the ability to open or close, whereas "Aleph" an ox-head 𐤀, denotes power or authority. Additionally, "Pey" represents a mouth 𐤐, implying the ability to speak, and "Aleph" 𐤀 again reinforces this authority. It's no coincidence that the letters that make up the name Kepha correspond to the powers granted to Simon in Matthew 16:19, "And I will give unto thee the keys of the kingdom of heaven; and whatsoever thou shalt bind on earth shall be bound in heaven; and whatsoever thou shalt loose on earth shall be loosed in heaven." Peter's name change to Kepha (in Greek Cephas) symbolizes a significant shift in Simon's identity and mission. But it doesn't stop there. When Jesus refers to him as Simon Barjona, it is not just a mere reference to his birth name or lineage; it invites us to investigate the profound significance of his name.

The name Simon, meaning "he has heard" or "God has heard," is coupled with "Barjona," translating to "son of Jonah." The Hebrew name Jonah means dove; more symbolically, this name translates to "son of the dove," unfolding layers of spiritual significance far beyond a mere familial association. In biblical symbolism, especially as revealed by

165

Matthew, the dove represents the Holy Spirit, as vividly illustrated at Jesus' baptism, where the Spirit descends like a dove. Therefore, calling Simon "Barjona" intertwines him with the imagery of the dove, suggesting a deeper, spiritual sonship—a connection to the Spirit Himself.

This appellation, then, highlights a divine revelation and spiritual hearing. Simon Peter's recognition of Jesus as the Christ doesn't stem from demonic revelation or human insight ("flesh and blood") but is a truth unveiled to him by "my Father which is in heaven." This moment transcends human wisdom, pointing to a direct impartation of knowledge from the Divine.

Thus, when Jesus addresses Simon as "Barjona," He is not merely citing his earthly father's name but signaling an extraordinary spiritual insight. He emphasizes that Peter's recognition of His divine identity is evidence of having "heard" from God, marking him as a "son of the Spirit." This distinction sets the stage for Peter's foundational role in the early Church, grounded not in his human capacity but in his receptivity to divine revelation.

In this light, the name Simon Barjona becomes a testament to the transformative power of divine revelation, affirming that true understanding of Jesus' identity as "the Son of God" is a gift from above,

166

accessible not through human reasoning but through the Spirit's revelation. This understanding underscores the intimate, spiritual relationship that followers of Jesus are called into—a relationship where hearing God's voice and receiving His revelation marks us as spiritual descendants, or "sons of God." This is reiterated in Romans 8:14, where Paul writes, "For as many as are led by the Spirit of God, they are the sons of God."

The devils recognition of Jesus as the "Son of God" also emphasizes the stark contrast between the kingdom of God and the kingdom of darkness. While the forces of darkness recognize and tremble before Jesus' divine authority, His ministry of teaching, healing, and liberating those oppressed by evil powers embodies the manifest kingdom of God. This dynamic confrontation between Jesus and demonic forces illustrates the ultimate authority of Jesus' divine sonship, highlighting His role as the conqueror of sin and death, the bearer of light into darkness, and the definitive manifestation of God's love and power.

The acknowledgment of Jesus as the "Son of God" by the forces of darkness throughout the Gospels is a powerful testament to His divine identity and authority. These encounters, while revealing the spiritual realm's recognition of Jesus' sovereignty, underscore the profound mystery of the Incarnation: God becoming man to redeem creation from sin and evil. The name "Son of God," as understood by devils, encapsulates the inconceivable vastness and significance of Jesus' mission, affirming His role as the preeminent bearer of redemption, the Light of the World, and the ultimate victor over the powers of darkness.

Old Testament Allusions to the Son of God

The Old Testament, while primarily focused on the covenant relationship between God and Israel, contains several verses that mention or allude to the concept of God having a son. These references are often messianic in nature, pointing towards a future anointed figure who would come to fulfill God's promises. Christians have interpreted some of these passages as precursors or prophecies regarding Jesus Christ, viewing him as the Son of God in a unique and divine sense. Here are some key Old Testament mentions and allusions to the concept:

Within God's covenant with David, He says, "I will be his father, and he shall be my son" (2 Samuel 7:14). This promise to David about his descendants, specifically Solomon in the immediate context, carries a deeper messianic significance as it points towards an eternal kingdom through David's line, which Christians interpret as fulfilled in Jesus.

The psalmist declares, "I will tell of the decree: The Lord said to me, you are my Son; today I have begotten you" (Psalm 2:7). People have interpreted this verse, which is part of a coronation psalm, as referring to the Davidic king and, consequently, to the Messiah. Acts 13:33 and Hebrews 5:5 in the New Testament directly apply this verse to Jesus, highlighting His divine sonship.

In Proverbs 30:4 rhetorical questions are posed about the nature of God and His works, including, "What is His name, and what is His son's name? Surely you know!" (Proverbs 30:4) While not directly prophetic, this verse has intrigued many as to its implication of divine sonship and has been seen by some as the concrete evidence needed to confirm that the Old Testament alludes to the fact that God, from the beginning, has had a son.

As previously revealed, in Isaiah's prophecy, unto us a child is born, unto us a son is given, who will have the government upon His shoulder and is called "Wonderful Counselor, Mighty God, Everlasting Father, Prince of Peace." (Isaiah 9:6) This is a direct prophecy of Jesus, highlighting attributes that align with divine sonship.

In the miraculous story of Shadrach, Meshach, and Abednego, Nebuchadnezzar sees a fourth figure in the fiery furnace whom he describes as, "The form of the fourth is like the Son of God." (Daniel 3:25) This phrase further strengthens the concept of God having a son.

Some have interpreted it as a theophany, implying a divine figure closely associated with God.

These Old Testament passages, among others, contribute to the messianic expectation of divine sonship that Christians see as fulfilled in our Lord Jesus Christ. Although Jewish interpretations of these texts do not view the Messiah as the divine Son of God in the same manner as we do, these verses serve as a foundation for understanding the New Testament's claims about Jesus' unique sonship. The Old Testament's hint at God's sonship serves as a foreshadowing, suggesting a Father-Son relationship between God and the promised Messiah.

This is My Son

The Father's declarations of Jesus as His Son are pivotal moments that affirm Jesus' unique identity, divine mission, and the nature of His relationship with the Father. These instances are not merely descriptive but serve foundational theological purposes, delineating Jesus' role within the Christian faith as the Messiah and the incarnate Word of God.

At Jesus' baptism, the heavens open as a voice declares, "This is my beloved Son, with whom I am well pleased" (Matthew 3:17). This event marks the beginning of Jesus' public ministry, with the divine affirmation acting as a celestial endorsement of His mission. The voice from heaven not only identifies Jesus as the Son but also expresses the Father's pleasure in Him, setting the tone for Jesus' redemptive work.

The transfiguration of Jesus is another moment of divine affirmation, where Peter, James, and John witness Jesus' divine glory. Again, a voice from the cloud proclaims, "This is my beloved Son, with whom I am well pleased; listen to him" (Matthew 17:5), which sounds eerily similar to Exodus 23:20–21. This instance underscores Jesus' authority and preeminence, urging His followers to heed His teachings, reinforcing His role as the mediator between God and humanity.

In the Gospel of John, there is a unique instance where Jesus speaks of God's testimony about Him, indicating a divine affirmation of His sonship and mission. While not a direct voice from heaven like in baptism or transfiguration, Jesus mentions that the Father has testified about Him (John 5:37), underscoring the continuous divine witness to His identity throughout His ministry.

These proclamations are theologically significant, as they highlight the intimate and unique relationship between Jesus and God, distinguishing Jesus from prophets and angels. By calling Jesus "My Son," God not only affirms His divine nature but also the incarnation— God becoming flesh to dwell among humanity (John 1:14). This divine sonship entails more than an identifier; it encompasses Jesus' role in

171

salvation, His authority to reveal God, and His sacrificial love demonstrated through His life, death, and resurrection.

God calling Jesus "His Son" is thus central to Christian doctrine, emphasizing Jesus' divinity, His mission of salvation, and His eternal relationship with the Father, inviting believers into a transformative relationship with God through faith in His Son.

God With Us

The name Immanuel, rooted in the Hebrew tradition, carries profound theological significance and directly connects to the identity of Jesus as the Son of God. Originating from the Hebrew words "Immanu" (עִמָּנוּ) meaning "with us" and "El" (אֵל) meaning "God," Immanuel beautifully encapsulates the promise of God's presence among His people. This name, translating to "God with us," emerges within a rich tapestry of prophecy, expectation, and divine revelation, offering deep insight into the Hebraic understanding of God's intimate relationship with humanity.

In Isaiah 7:14, amid political turmoil and the threat of invasion, the prophet Isaiah delivers a message of hope to King Ahaz of Judah, marking the prophetic announcement of Immanuel. Isaiah prophesies that a virgin will conceive and give birth to a son named Immanuel, signifying

172

God's enduring presence and support for His people, even in times of distress. This prophecy is emblematic of the broader biblical theme that God is not a distant deity but is intimately involved in the lives of His people, guiding, protecting, and saving them.

The Gospel of Matthew (1:23) explicitly connects the prophecy of Immanuel to the birth of Jesus Christ, interpreting Jesus' birth as the fulfillment of Isaiah's words. Matthew's use of the name Immanuel to describe Jesus serves as a theological declaration that, in Jesus, God has indeed come to dwell among humanity. Jesus' ministry, miracles, teachings, and ultimately, His sacrificial death and resurrection embody the reality of God's presence with us. Jesus makes tangible the abstract concept of God's proximity, demonstrating God's love and commitment to the redemption and restoration of humanity.

This correlation between Immanuel and Jesus profoundly underscores the Christian understanding of Jesus as the Son of God. It affirms the incarnation as the ultimate expression of God's desire to be with His people—a theme deeply embedded in the Hebraic tradition but brought to its full revelation in the person of Jesus. As Immanuel, Jesus embodies the fulfillment of God's promises throughout the Hebrew Scriptures, bridging the gap between the divine and the human and offering a new way for people to experience God's presence.

Furthermore, the name Immanuel, in its declaration of "God with us," provides a foundational basis for the Christian faith. It reassures believers of God's immanent presence in our lives, accessible through Jesus, the Son of God. This name not only affirms Jesus' divinity but also His role as the mediator between God and humanity, fulfilling the longing for reconciliation and communion with the divine.

In essence, Immanuel encapsulates the heart of the Christian message: in Jesus, God has come to dwell with His people, providing hope, salvation, and the promise of eternal fellowship. This life-changing truth, anchored in the name Immanuel and its fulfillment in Jesus, continues to inspire faith, worship, and a deeper understanding of God's love and presence in the world.

The Son of the Lord

In the intricate layers of Jewish interpretive tradition, the Targumim—Aramaic translation of the Hebrew Bible—hold a unique place, bridging the ancient text with the lived experiences and theological inquiries of Jewish communities. Among these, the Targum Neofiti offers a fascinating glimpse into the Jewish understanding of divine communication and presence. Particularly, its use of "Memra" (Aramaic: מימרא, Word) as a conduit for divine action and revelation invites a deeper exploration into the concept of "the Son of the Lord," especially as it

174

resonates with the Genesis creation narrative and the broader biblical motif of divine sonship.

In Genesis, the act of creation is initiated through the spoken word: "God said, 'Let there be light,' and there was light." The Targum Neofiti richly amplifies this passage, foundational to the Judeo-Christian understanding of God as Creator, by inserting "Memra," a translation that emphasizes God's word not just as speech, but as an agent of creation itself. The Targum renders this act of speaking as the Memra of the Lord bringing forth light, imbuing the text with a sense of divine agency and presence that transcends the mere verbal.

We understand the Aramaic term "Memra" as the creative word of God, a manifestation of His will and purpose. But in the Targum Neofiti, it's used in a way that goes beyond language or literature. It represents the idea that God's word is a separate but unified part of Himself, which is similar to how John described Jesus as the Logos, or "Word made flesh." The Targumic portrayal of Memra reflects an intuitive grasp of divine sonship, where Memra acts as the executor of God's will, mirroring the relationship between a father and his son, where the son carries out the father's commands, embodying his authority and essence.

The elucidation of Memra as "the Son of the Lord" within the Targum Neofiti picks up on the foundational concept of sonship present

175

from the very beginning of the biblical text. "Bar" in "Bereshit," suggestive of the Son at the heart of creation, finds a parallel in the Targum's Memra, which serves as a mediating presence, executing the will of God in the material world. This understanding of Memra aligns with the nuanced biblical portrayal of divine sonship, not merely as a title or a status but as an active, relational dynamic between the Creator and His divine word or wisdom.

The concept of "the Son of the Lord," as illuminated through the lens of Memra, offers a profound insight into the Jewish conceptual framework for understanding God's interaction with creation. It suggests a mode of divine action that is both immanent and transcendent, personal yet all-encompassing—a way of conceiving God's presence that anticipates the Christian revelation of Jesus as the Son of God. In the Memra, we find a theological precursor to the New Testament Logos, where the Word not only speaks or commands but enters into creation, embodying God's salvific will and purpose.

In In this context, the Targum Neofiti's interpretation of Genesis does more than translate; it theologically recasts the creation narrative to highlight the active and personal nature of God's word. This recasting not only enriches the Jewish understanding of God's relationship with the world, as found through Aramaic, it also dialogues with the Christian concept of the Incarnation, where the Word becomes flesh and dwells among us. The Memra of the Lord, understood as "the Son of the Lord," encapsulates a shared heritage of monotheistic faiths—a vision of divine word and wisdom that bridges heaven and earth, transcending the confines of language to touch the mystery of God's ongoing act of creation and revelation.

Thus, the Targum Neofiti's rendering of Memra as an expression of divine sonship enriches our understanding of biblical themes of word, wisdom, and sonship. The concept of God's communicative and creative action through His Word finds its ultimate expression in the Christian doctrine of the Incarnation. Through this lens, the Memra serves as a bridge, a theological touchstone that invites believers of different traditions to explore the rich, complex, and nuanced understandings of God's word as a living, active presence in the world, executing His will and drawing all of creation into a deeper relationship with the Creator.

When we consider the profound significance of the name "Son of God," we come across a designation that appears to grant Jesus unparalleled distinction and uniqueness. However, even within this lofty name, we find the need for a distinguishing qualifier—"the only begotten Son." This exclusive descriptor, which distinguishes Jesus as the one and only Son of God, emphasizes His unique relationship with the Father.

While the name "Son of God" appears to confer supreme honor, the addition of "only begotten" emphasizes Jesus' preeminence, making Him unparalleled in His divine sonship. Thus, while "Son of God" may denote an elevated status, the qualifier "only begotten" ensures that Jesus stands out as uniquely deserving of adoration and reverence. As a result, the name "Son of God," while conveying unparalleled majesty, falls short of claiming ultimate supremacy, giving rise to the revelation of a "name above all names."

Chapter Nine

KING OF KINGS
& LORD OF LORDS

T he name "King of Kings and Lord of Lords" attributed to Jesus Christ has had an astonishing depth of biblical and theological significance, echoing throughout Scripture from the Old Testament to the New. This double name honors Jesus' unparalleled sovereignty and command over all creation, while also bringing to life the richness of messianic prophecy, divine worship, and revelation.

In the Hebrew Scriptures, the theme of divine supremacy is dominant. The Psalms and Prophets beautifully express God as the supreme ruler of the universe. For example, Psalm 47:2 exclaims, "For the Lord Most High is awesome, the great King over all the earth." Such declarations set the divine stage for the coming Messiah, envisioned as God's sovereign on earth. Daniel 7:13–14 vividly depicts the gift of everlasting dominion to "one like the Son of man," suggesting a messiah with universal rule deeply ingrained in Jewish hope.

The New Testament reveals Jesus as the Messiah, who not only fulfills but embodies these ancient prophecies. Matthew's Gospel meticulously traces Jesus' lineage from Abraham to David, integrating Him into Israel's royal lineage and messianic prophecies. This genealogy not only confirms Jesus' Jewish identity but also asserts His divine right to David's throne, which is consistent with God's promise of an eternal kingdom to David. The reference in Revelation 5:5 to Jesus as the "Lion of the tribe of Judah" emphasizes His messianic role by connecting Him to the tribe associated with kingship.

The Book of Revelation establishes Jesus' identity as the "King of Kings and Lord of Lords." Revelation 17:14 foretells His triumph over earthly rulers, while Revelation 19:16 intriguingly reveals the writing of "a name," not plural names, on His thigh, revealing His eternal reign. Such verses depict Jesus as the fulfillment of Israel's messianic hopes and the ruler of all powers, both earthly and heavenly.

*And he hath on his vesture and on his thigh **a name** written, KING OF KINGS, AND LORD OF LORDS. (Revelation 19:16)*

This double name is more than just an honorific; it captures the essence of Christian faith—Jesus' divinity and His reign over all creation. Philippians 2:9–11 reflects on His divine exaltation and encourages all creation to accept Jesus as Lord. The Old Testament affirms God's unique sovereignty, now fully revealed in Jesus.

Furthermore, "King of Kings and Lord of Lords" offers hope for Jesus' second coming, envisioning a world where He fully reveals His kingship, thereby fulfilling the prophets' visions of peace, justice, and righteousness under His benign rule. The Bible portrays Jesus as the "King of Kings and Lord of Lords," illustrating a dominion similar to David's based not on force but on love, sacrifice, and righteousness. Jesus' kingship redefines power, laying the groundwork for the Christian life and hope.

Surpassing Messiah

The name "King of Kings and Lord of Lords" elevates Jesus above even the esteemed Messiah. While "Messiah" represents the long-awaited liberator in Jewish tradition, "King of Kings and Lord of Lords" extends His authority to the entire universe, confirming His dominion over all creation.

Judaism's messianic vision called for a deliverer to save Israel and usher in a period of peace. This vision, vividly depicted in Isaiah and Jeremiah, foresaw a Davidic descendant as the anointed savior. However, "King of Kings and Lord of Lords" goes beyond these nationalistic and religious boundaries, heralding Jesus' rule over all powers and authorities.

Revelation vividly depicts Jesus, the Lamb, as the victor over evil, with His eternal sovereignty declared over the universe. These titles declare Jesus' lordship to be limitless, emphasizing not only His salvific role but also His supremacy and divinity.

This cosmic rule is central to Christian eschatology, as it promises Jesus' ultimate victory and the restoration of creation under His just reign. It asserts that no power can challenge Jesus' authority, anchoring the Christian faith and worship in His all-encompassing lordship.

Though "Messiah" remains important, referring to Jesus' fulfillment of prophecies and role as Savior, "King of Kings and Lord of Lords" takes this understanding to a cosmic level, presenting Jesus as the sovereign ruler of all, central to God's plan for universal redemption.

Eclipsing Earthly Rulers

In Scripture, the titles "King of Kings" and "Lord of Lords" contrast the might of earthly rulers like Nebuchadnezzar and Artaxerxes with God's and Jesus' divine authority. While these monarchs represent the pinnacle of human governance, divine titles denote an eternal and sovereign rule that one-up and far outstrip any earthly authority.

Nebuchadnezzar, called "king of kings" in Ezekiel, exemplifies vast imperial control; however, when applied to our heavenly Father and Jesus, this title transcends earthly dominion to represent supreme, everlasting authority over the universe. Revelation vividly depicts this elevation, praising Jesus as the Lamb who overcomes, establishing His reign as eternal and unrivaled by any temporal power. Specific biblical contexts share this divine sovereignty, but its application to the Father and Jesus is significantly different from that of earthly kings. For Nebuchadnezzar and Artaxerxes, the title "king of kings" represented the pinnacle of human achievement and power. But, when attributed to the Father and the Son, it signifies a dominion that stretches throughout creation, characterized not by force but by justice, love, and righteousness.

The scriptural journey from human kings to Jesus' divine kingship demonstrates a shift in our understanding of power. Earthly kings, with their finite reigns, serve as counterpoints to Jesus' eternal kingship, which promises not only victory over sin and death but also hope for a restored world under His just and loving rule.

This divine kingship prompts believers to reconsider the nature of power and authority. It invites us into a relationship with a King whose rule is characterized by sacrificial love and who welcomes us into His kingdom as co-heirs rather than subjects. Jesus, as the "King of Kings and Lord of Lords," represents the pinnacle of divine authority, inviting all creation to participate in a story of redemption that culminates in His eternal reign.

Thus, the double name "King of Kings and Lord of Lords" is more than just accolades; it captures the essence of the Christian message: the revelation of God's supreme power in our Lord Jesus Christ. A name that invites us to see Jesus as more than just a historical figure, but as the living embodiment of God's promise to humanity. The entire narrative of the Scriptures culminates in Jesus, who offers a vision of a world redeemed and united under the benevolent rule of the ultimate Sovereign.

As we consider the awe-inspiring name "King of Kings and Lord of Lords," we are drawn into the grandeur of its proclamation and the majestic sovereignty it represents. However, our quest for the ultimate name reveals that, although "King of Kings" signifies regal supremacy, Jesus is not the sole recipient of this name. Throughout history, earthly rulers such as Nebuchadnezzar and Artaxerxes have worn this majestic title, basking in its splendor and authority. However, Jesus goes beyond mere earthly kingship by adding "Lord of Lords," a divine name that distinguishes Him as supreme over all rulers, earthly and celestial alike. Thus, while "King of Kings and Lord of Lords" alludes to a revelation beyond human comprehension, it stops short of asserting ultimate supremacy of "the name above all names."

Chapter Ten

THE LIVING WORD

A t the heart of Christian theology is a profound and astounding concept: the Word of God, known as the Logos, taking on human form in our Lord Jesus Christ. In John's Gospel's poetic prologue, Greek philosophical concepts blend seamlessly with the Hebrew tradition's deep relational understanding of God. This union focuses on the intricacies of divine revelation and the profound dialogue between God and humanity. The Hebrew term "Dabar," which means both "word" and "thing," connects the philosophical and relational aspects of this dialogue, capturing the dynamic nature of God's interaction with humanity.

Hebraically, "Dabar" is more than just speech; it is a force that represents the ability to effect real-world change. This philosophy is consistent with John's introduction, portraying the Logos as God's active, creative force rather than simply divine rhetoric. The seamless parallel between "word" and "thing" in the term "Dabar" highlights the tangible, powerful reality of God's Word, which reaches its pinnacle with Jesus' Incarnation.

"And the Word became flesh and dwelt among us," declares John 1:14, presenting the Incarnation as the ultimate embodiment of "Dabar." Jesus, the Word made flesh, embodies divine intention and action, uniting the divine and the human, the abstract and the concrete. This convergence challenges our understandings of communication and presence, presenting Jesus as the definitive, approachable revelation of God to humanity.

The Old Testament lays the groundwork for this idea, highlighting the "Dabar YHWH" (the Word of the Lord) was God's active presence throughout history. Prophets such as Ezekiel, who frequently stated that "Dabar Adonai YHWH," or "The word of the Lord came unto me," served as vessels for God's Word, ushering in change and direction. This tradition of the Word as both revelation and transformation prepares the grounds for John's profound claim: the Word became flesh.

One of the most misunderstood verses in the Bible is John 3:13, where Jesus declares, "And no man hath ascended up to heaven, but he that came down from heaven, even the Son of Man which is in heaven." (John 3:13 KJV) Many Bible readers interpret Jesus' statement as denying the presence of any man in heaven, but this interpretation is inaccurate. A closer look reveals the subtleties in Jesus' words. We can clarify this by comparing Enoch and Elijah's experiences to Jesus' statement. According to Genesis 5:24, "God took" Enoch into heaven, while Elijah ascended into heaven by a "chariot of fire and whirlwind." Acts 1:9–12, on the other hand, explicitly declares Jesus' "taking up" without specifying the method, subtly suggesting that no one or nothing took Him; He did it by Himself. Unlike Enoch and Elijah, who never returned from their experiences, Jesus descended from heaven, ascended, and will descend again. Thus, Jesus' statement in John 3:13 emphasizes His unique status as the Word made flesh, the only man who can descend and ascend at will—the embodiment of God's commandment on earth, His word running swiftly (Psalm 147:15, KJV).

The book of Deuteronomy, also known as "Dabarim" (Words), serves as an intriguing bridge between the Testaments. This collection of Moses' teachings emphasizes the life-giving value of adhering to God's Word. During His wilderness temptation, Jesus aligned Himself with Deuteronomy, embodying the Law and Prophets and becoming the living "Dabar" (Matthew 4:1–11). His application of the law in Matthew 5:17–18 goes beyond mere legal compliance, illuminating its complexities and guiding believers to a richer, more complete embrace of God's will. Jesus' role goes beyond conventional interpretations, intensifying the law's demands through His life and teachings.

Thus, Jesus' Incarnation as the Word that became flesh represents a divine initiative to engage and redeem humanity. In Jesus, the "Dabar" (Word) becomes tangible, making the unseen God visible and accessible. This mystery invites believers to encounter God not in abstract terms but through the person of Jesus, who represents divine love, wisdom, and salvation. The Incarnation invites us to have an intimate relationship with the living God through His Word, which speaks directly to our hearts.

Luke 1:35 further highlights and aligns Jesus with "Dabar" by referring to Him as the "holy thing" born of Mary, adding to its theological depth. This announcement combines the concept of "Dabar" with the miraculous, as the Word not only communicates divinely but also manifests as the divine "holy thing" in Jesus Christ Himself.

This insight broadens our understanding of "Dabar," which depicts God's Word as an active, incarnate reality that shapes the universe and history. Jesus, as the fulfillment of "Dabar," personifies God's redemptive narrative, connecting creation, revelation, and prophecy in His person.

The Voice and Angel of the LORD

Genesis and Exodus reveal "the voice of the Lord" and "the angel of the LORD" as precursors to the Incarnation. These theophanies—God's voice in Eden and His messenger—foreshadow Jesus' arrival as the Word made flesh, demonstrating God's evolving revelation and desire to commune with humanity.

Contrary to popular belief and imagery, the Hebrew term "angel" (mal'âk) does not necessarily refer to a winged being with a halo above its head who dwells in heaven. Rather, it signifies the dispatch of someone or something as a deputy or messenger, often serving as God's ambassador or spokesperson. While winged creatures are depicted in the Bible, they are usually specifically referred to as Cherubim, Seraphim, or other heavenly beings rather than simply being called "angels" unless he is speaking on behalf of the LORD. Thus, when we encounter references to an "angel of the LORD," it is more accurate to interpret him as a messenger of the LORD—an emissary speaking on His behalf, coming as His voice, and embodying His authority.

The depiction of the "voice of the LORD" seeking Adam and Eve in Genesis 3 and "the angel of the LORD" leading Israel in Exodus 23 foreshadow Jesus, the Word, who seeks and saves the lost while guiding believers to the truth. Jesus embodies these manifestations, bringing God's voice and presence to the world in a new and unprecedented way.

In the narrative of Genesis 16, we are introduced to the enigmatic figure of "the angel of the LORD," who makes a groundbreaking declaration to Hagar: "I will multiply your seed." This statement, notably using "I" rather than attributing the action to the LORD, peels back layers of mystery surrounding the angel of the LORD's true identity. This celestial messenger not only commands Hagar to name her son Ishmael, signifying "God has heard," but also compels Hagar to bestow upon God a name unprecedented in biblical history: El Roi (אל ראי). Hagar's act of naming God El Roi marks the first instance in Scripture where a human assigns a name to the divine.

Contrary to the common interpretation of "the God who sees," El Roi more accurately captures "the God who appeared," illuminating the angel of the LORD as the tangible presence of the invisible God. This interpretation gains further clarity from Hagar's experience, as naming Him "the God who sees" does not align with the context of her encounter. El Roi, then, encapsulates God's revelation and visible manifestation of Himself to Hagar, an insight affirmed when the word raah (רָאָה) is used to describe the LORD's appearance to Abraham in Genesis 17:1. Through Hagar's profound encounter and the bestowed name, we are invited to understand the angel of the LORD not just as a messenger but as a divine presence made visible, offering a glimpse into the depth of God's willingness to reveal Himself to those in despair.

With the Old Testament's visible manifestations of God in mind, the Incarnation becomes more than just a theological concept; it is at the heart of God's pursuit of humanity, which culminates in Jesus, the ultimate messenger of divine love and salvation. Jesus, as the living "Dabar," invites us into a transformative relationship with God, bridging the gap between the Creator and His creation and providing a direct encounter with His love. The eternal Word speaks anew through Jesus, inviting us to engage in a living dialogue with God, unlike the dumb (voiceless) idols of other nations.

This direct encounter with Jesus, the incarnate Word, changes our perception of divine communication, transforming it from just an idea to a lived experience. Through Him, the abstract becomes intimate, and the infinite becomes personal. The Word made flesh is God's ultimate invitation to humanity to interact with Him as a present, loving entity rather than a distant force.

The profound implications of the Incarnation permeate the very fabric of Christian life and worship. Jesus sees, touches, and follows the Word, not just hears it. He is the embodiment of God's promises, the tangible manifestation of divine love, and the means of eternal communion with the Creator. His life exemplifies the ideal response to

God's Word, and His teachings help believers live out the result of this divine-human encounter.

Furthermore, Jesus' resurrection and ascension are not the end of this encounter, rather it continues through the Holy Spirit. The Comforter, as promised by Jesus, keeps the presence of the Word alive within the Christian community, allowing believers to live in constant communion with God. The name "Comforter," derived from the Greek word "paraklētos," which means "advocate" or "counselor," takes on a deeper significance when viewed through its Latin roots. In Latin, "Comforter" combines "com," meaning "with," and "fort," which means "strength" or "power." Thus, like Jesus, the Holy Spirit is revealed to be another "with power." Such insight is made evident in passages like Luke 24:49 and Acts 1:8, in which believers are promised power from above. Through the Holy Spirit, the church is empowered to be Christ's body on earth, embodying the Word made flesh through acts of love, service, and witness.

The Incarnation also sheds new light on the Scriptures, encouraging believers to read and interpret it through the lens of Jesus' life and teachings. As the Word made flesh, Jesus is the key to comprehending the breadth and depth of God's revelation. Every story, prophecy, and law in Scripture is fulfilled in Him, demonstrating the unity and coherence of God's plan for salvation. The Scriptures are no longer a collection of ancient texts but rather a dynamic, living dialogue between God and humanity, centered on our Lord Jesus Christ.

By accepting Jesus as the Word made flesh, we are invited into a relationship that transcends time and space and is founded on the reality of God's unchanging love and purpose. This relationship is active, not passive, and invites believers to participate in God's redemptive work in this world. Christians are called to be messengers of the Gospel, embodying Jesus' love, grace, and truth in all aspects of their lives.

The concept of the Word made flesh thus captures the essence of the Christian faith: God's love manifested in our Lord Jesus Christ, inviting all of creation into a loving, redeeming, and transformative relationship. Constant revelation of this mystery deepens believers' understanding of God, the universe, and ourselves. Through the Incarnation, God's eternal Word speaks directly to all people's hearts, inviting us into a transformative, empowering, and redeeming relationship with the living God.

The Incarnation of Jesus as the Word made flesh is not only a cornerstone of Christianity but also the beating heart of our identity and purpose. It challenges and inspires believers to embody the reality of God's Word in the world. God's voice continues to echo through the ages through Jesus, the living Word, inviting all to participate in a story of divine love and purpose that transforms the world—one life at a time.

The Trinity of Witnesses

The Scriptures reveal a deeper divine reality, which includes the profound mystery of the Incarnation, where the Word became flesh. John's first epistle provides a glimpse into the celestial realm, introducing a divine testimony that goes beyond human comprehension: "For there are three that bear witness in heaven: the Father, the Word, and the Holy Spirit, and these three are one." (1 John 5:7) This passage not only reaffirms the profound truth of the Incarnation, but it also expands our understanding of divine witness by presenting the Word as an essential component of the three that bear witness to God's redemptive plan for mankind.

The Word, known to us through the Incarnation as Jesus, exists in perfect harmony with the Father and the Holy Spirit. This three-part testimony emphasizes the interconnectedness of God's nature and His revelation to humanity. The Father, as the source of all that exists, sent the Word to become flesh, bridging the infinite gap between the divine and the human. The Holy Spirit, who proceeds from the Father and the Son, continues to instill this truth in the hearts of all believers, guiding us to all truth and sustaining us on our faith journey.

In this heavenly testimony, the Word is the living bridge, the mediator who reveals the Father to us (John 14:6–9). Jesus, as the Word, represents God's creative power, wisdom, and love, revealing the invisible God to the human eye. Through His life, death, and resurrection, He reveals God's character and will definitively, offering Himself as the ultimate proof of God's love and the way to salvation.

The work of the Spirit, confirms with our spirit that we are God's children, mirrors the unity of the Father, the Word, and the Holy Spirit in heaven in the believer's experience (Romans 8:16). This divine testimony is not a distant reality but rather a present and active force within the Christianity, empowering us to live in accordance with God's truth and to bear witness to the gospel of our Lord Jesus Christ.

The inclusion of "the Word" in the heavenly witness highlights the ongoing nature of divine revelation and interaction with humanity. Just as the Word was present at the creation of the world, speaking life into existence, He is still active in the world through the Holy Spirit, speaking to our hearts and drawing us closer to God. Combining the Word's ongoing activity with the Father and the Spirit reveals a dynamic, living God, deeply invested in His creation and dedicated to our redemption and restoration. Thus, the testimony of the Father, the Word, and the Holy Spirit serves as the foundation for Christian faith and assurance of salvation. It is a testimony that spans time and space, uniting the Christian community throughout the ages in a shared confession and hope. As believers, we find strength in this heavenly witness to face life's trials and challenges, anchored in our knowledge of God's love and faithfulness.

Recognizing "the Word" as one of heaven's three witnesses also invites us to delve deeper into the mystery of God's nature and redemptive work. It invites us to look beyond the limits of our comprehension and embrace the infinite, living truth of a God who desires to reveal Himself to each of us. The Father, the Word, and the Holy Spirit draw us into a narrative of divine love that shapes our identity, guides our path, and assures us of our place in God's eternal kingdom. This revelation of the Word as part of the heavenly three broadens our understanding of the Incarnation and its implications for our faith and life. The larger narrative of God's purpose and action in the world reveals Jesus, the Word made flesh. Reflecting on the mystery of our triune God invites us to live in the light of this divine testimony, demonstrating the Gospel's truth through our words and actions, and actively participating in the unfolding of God's redemptive plan for all creation. The Christian community continues to testify to the hope and salvation found in our Lord Jesus Christ, the living Word, who bridges heaven and earth, inviting all people into the embrace of God's eternal love.

The deep significance of the name "Living Word" draws us in with its allusion to divine revelation and eternal truth. This name takes us to the heart of God's communication with humanity. But, despite its splendor, we see a subtle ambiguity in its use throughout Scripture. While it represents the dynamic and life-giving nature of God's Word, it also brings to mind images of messengers or voices who deliver divine messages, blurring the line between the divine and the human. Indeed, the portrayal of figures like Malachi and other messengers of the Lord suggests an inextricable connection between the divine Word and its messengers. Thus, while "Living Word" evokes divine power and authority, its association with human messengers adds a layer of complexity that prevents it from asserting ultimate supremacy. It is a profound revelation of God's ongoing communication with His creation, but it falls short of capturing the fullness of the "name above all names." Instead, it serves as the forerunner to the revelation of the name that encompasses the entirety of divine sovereignty and reigns unrivaled for all eternity.

Chapter Eleven

THE NAME ABOVE ALL NAMES

This journey through the Scriptures has revealed an incredibly theological saga that has spanned from creation to the revelation of God's eternal plan. Amidst this divine narrative, a surprising revelation emerges: the name heralded as "above all names" is not, as many believe, Jesus. This realization challenges conventional understanding and invites a deeper investigation into the essence of divine revelation.

While the name Jesus, or Yeshua in Hebrew, has powerful meaning, expressing "YHWH is salvation," it does not stand as the name above all names. The name Jesus, rich in meaning and redemptive hope, serves as a bridge between humanity and YHWH's salvific power, rather than the ultimate point of divine identification.

It is a common misconception, fueled by the name's widespread recognition and veneration, to associate Jesus with the supreme "name above all names." However, this viewpoint ignores the critical fact that the name Jesus represents the revelation of YHWH's saving grace, not an assertion of the holder's exclusivity among divine titles.

The Scripture paints a complex portrait of Jesus, celebrating His divine nature, eternal preexistence, and the mystery of the Incarnation, all of which highlight the interconnected reality of Jesus and YHWH. In this light, Jesus appears not as the pinnacle of God's names, but as a clear demonstration of YHWH's redemptive engagement with the world.

This understanding encourages believers to reconsider their preconceptions, recognizing that our emphasis on the earthly name "Jesus" reflects not just its exaltation, but also our deep devotion to the one who embodies YHWH's salvation. As we read through the Bible, we gain a deeper, more nuanced appreciation for the divine names, seeing Jesus as a key figure in the grand, ongoing revelation of YHWH's love and purpose for creation.

At the heart of this journey is the realization that Jesus has always used the name YHWH, to present God's self-existence and eternal nature. The Gospel of John begins with a profound statement about Jesus as the Word: "In the beginning was the Word, and the Word was with God, and the Word was God" (John 1:1). This passage emphasizes Jesus' divine nature and active participation in creation, confirming His preexistence and role as a co-creator alongside the Father. In Genesis 1:26, "Let us make man in our image, after our likeness," the plural form Elohim implies divine plurality within God's unity, providing insight into the complex nature of the Godhead and Jesus' integral role within it.

This divine plurality, which is present throughout the creation narrative, finds resonance in the New Testament, where Jesus' statements such as "If you've seen me, you've seen the Father" (John 14:9) and descriptions of Him as "the express image of His [God's] person" (Hebrews 1:3) emphasize His unique revelation of God to humanity. These declarations not only emphasize Jesus' unity with the Father but also His role as a tangible manifestation of the invisible God, connecting the finite and the infinite.

Yesh

The name YHWH, which reveals God as the self-existent One, immediately emphasizes Jesus' transcendence and eternal being. The name Jesus—Yeshua in Hebrew, where "Yesh" represents existence—subtly encodes this concept of preexistence. This linguistic connection, which echoes the divine name I AM (Ehyeh), represents Jesus' eternal nature and His continuity with the God who revealed Himself to Moses as "I AM WHO I AM" (Exodus 3:14). The Hebrew word "Yesh" (יֵשׁ) has a profound place in the linguistic and spiritual landscape of Hebraic thought, meaning "exists" or "is present." This term goes beyond the simple acknowledgement of existence; it encapsulates the essence of being and presence in the world. In a variety of contexts, from mundane confirmations of presence to deep philosophical assertions about life and hope, "yesh" serves as a foundational affirmation, meaning "there is" or "there are."

When used in everyday conversation, "yesh" confirms the existence of objects, people, or situations. For example, responding with "yesh" to the question "Is there a church nearby?" confirms the church's presence while also embedding a layer of existential recognition within this affirmation. This usage, while straightforward, speaks to a deeper understanding of the world around us and our interactions with it.

The name "Yeshua" (Jesus) amplifies the significance of "Yesh". This linguistic connection broadens our understanding of Jesus' identity and mission. "Yeshua," which means "The LORD is salvation," begins with the essence of existence, connecting Jesus' very name to the fundamental concept of divine presence and action in the world. This naming emphasizes the belief in Jesus as the embodiment of God's presence among humanity, a living testament to the idea that in Him the existential and the divine converge, providing hope and salvation and affirming God's active involvement in the fabric of life.

"Yesh" goes beyond its simple translation and becomes a term with multiple layers of meaning and implication. From confirming the existence of the mundane to expressing profound spiritual truths about hope and divine presence, "Yesh" captures the complexities of existence, ownership, and optimism. The connection between "Yesh" and the name "Yeshua" expands the theological and existential dimensions of Jesus' identity, portraying Him as the personification of divine presence, as well as a hopeful affirmation that "there is" salvation and presence in Him. The Hebrew language, through "Yesh," provides a lens through which to explore the nuanced interplay between existence, faith, and the divine, inviting reflection on the truths that shape our understanding of the world and our place within it.

Scripture inextricably links the phrase "in my name" or "in the name of" to the divine name YHWH, highlighting God's authority and presence in actions performed in His name. Jesus' use of this idiom, particularly in the Great Commission (Matthew 28:19) and prayers (John 17:5), demonstrates a strong identification with YHWH, emphasizing His divine authority and unity with the Father. Indeed, the term "Yesh" can also function as a cue to closely examine or monitor the individual bearing this name.

Yesh reveals that Jesus was given the name above all names, resulting in every knee bowing and every tongue confessing that He is Lord (Philippians 2:9–11), which is not an innovation but a fulfillment of the divine promise revealed in Scriptures such as Isaiah 45:23 and echoed throughout the New Testament. Acts 2:21 and Romans 10:13, which parallel Joel 2:32, vividly depict this fulfillment by proclaiming the salvific power of calling on the name of the Lord. These passages affirm that Jesus' name is YHWH, and they contain the ultimate revelation of God's nature and purpose.

The biblical narrative, from Genesis to Revelation, intricately presents Jesus as the preexistent Word, embodying the divine name YHWH, who reveals, expresses, and understands the fullness of God. This revelation calls believers to understand the depth of Jesus' identity as God incarnate, the King of Kings and Lord of Lords, who reveals the Father's heart through His life, death, and resurrection and invites humanity into an eternal relationship with the triune God. Jesus fully expresses and reveals the name YHWH, inviting all creation to worship the One who preexists the beginning and will continue to exist forever.

YHWH Hidden in Plain Sight

The New Testament's concealment and revelation of the divine name YHWH, commonly translated as "Lord" instead of all capitals "LORD," presents an intriguing study in biblical interpretation and theology. This subtle yet profound shift from Hebrew Scriptures to Greek New Testament manuscripts reflects both linguistic changes and theological continuity within the Christian canon. We can learn how the early Christian writers directly connected our Lord Jesus Christ to YHWH, the God of Israel, by examining passages quoted in the New Testament that originate from the Old Testament and clearly identify YHWH as "LORD."

Jewish tradition meticulously avoids the Tetragrammaton, YHWH, the most sacred name of God in the Hebrew Bible, replacing it in readings with "Adonai" (Lord) and HaShem. This practice influenced the Septuagint (LXX), the Greek translation of the Hebrew Scriptures, which renders YHWH as "Kyrios" (Lord). The Greek New Testament follows this convention, using "Kyrios" to refer to both the Old Testament's YHWH and to our Lord Jesus Christ. Although this linguistic shift obscures the specific name YHWH under the title "Lord," early Christians would have recognized the profound connections between Jesus and the God of Israel through the use of scripture and the application of this title.

Several passages in the New Testament explicitly quote Old Testament Scriptures containing the Tetragrammaton, applying them to Jesus and thus identifying Him with YHWH. For example, in Philippians 2:9–11, the Apostle Paul undoubtedly quotes Isaiah 45:23, in which God declares that every knee will bow before Him and every tongue will swear. Paul applies this declaration to Jesus, implying that Jesus is the one to whom every knee will bow, thereby identifying Jesus with God and YHWH.

Hebrews 1:10–12 provides another striking example, as the author applies Psalm 102:25–27, which originally praised YHWH as the immutable creator, to Jesus. This application emphasizes the early Christian understanding of Jesus as a participant in God's divine identity, sharing attributes and actions attributed solely to YHWH in the Hebrew Bible.

"Of old, thou laid the foundation of the earth; and the heavens are the work of thy hands. They shall perish, but thou shalt endure: yea, all of them shall wax old like a garment; as a vesture shalt thou change them, and they shall be changed: but thou art the same, and thy years shall have no end. "(Psalm 102:25–27)

"And, Thou, Lord, in the beginning hast laid the foundation of the earth; and the heavens are the works of thine hands: They shall perish; but thou remainest; and they all shall wax old as doth a garment; And as a vesture shalt thou fold them up, and they shall be changed: but thou art the same, and thy years shall not fail." (Hebrews 1:10–12)

Furthermore, the phrase "calling on the name of the Lord" in the New Testament supports this point. Joel 2:32 asserts that salvation awaits everyone who invokes the name of the LORD (YHWH). Acts 2:21 and Romans 10:13 repeat this prophecy, but in the New Testament context, "calling on the name of the Lord" refers to calling on Jesus, indicating that the early Christians saw Jesus as embodying YHWH's presence and power through Him.

The New Testament's use of "Lord" (Kyrios) in places where the Old Testament refers to YHWH is a theological statement rather than a linguistic artifact. It reflects the early Christian belief that Jesus possessed the identity and divine sovereignty of Israel's God. Jesus' use of "I am" statements in the Gospel of John, reminiscent of YHWH's self-revelation to Moses in Exodus 3:14, and titles like "the first and the last" in Revelation, mirroring divine appellations in Isaiah 41:4, 44:6, & 48:12 further support this.

The New Testament's concealment and revelation of YHWH reveals a complex theological continuity that links the New Testament Scriptures to its Hebrew roots. Through their inspired use of Old Testament references and titles, the apostolic authors present Jesus as the final revelation of YHWH, the God who was, is, and will come. This continuity does not simply equate Jesus with the Father but rather places Him within the complex unity of the Godhead, reinforcing the Christian doctrine of the Trinity.

LORD

Being made so much better than the angels, as he hath by inheritance obtained a more excellent name than they. For unto which of the angels said he at any time, Thou art my Son, this day have I begotten thee? And again, I will be to him a Father, and he shall be to me a Son? And again, when he bringeth in the firstbegotten into the world, he saith, And let all the angels of God worship him. (Hebrews 1:4-6, KJV)

Hebrews 1:4-6 provides compelling biblical evidence for Jesus' identity as the embodiment of YHWH, the sacred name traditionally rendered as "LORD" in English Old Testament translations. Hebrews emphasizes Jesus' superiority over angels, highlighting His divine status and authority, inextricably linked to the name YHWH. Let us look at how these verses support the theological revelation that Jesus is the embodiment of YHWH's presence, power, and promise.

Hebrews 1:4 says, "Being made so much better than the angels, as he hath by inheritance obtained a more excellent name than they." This verse sets the tone by emphasizing Jesus' exalted position, which surpasses even the angels. The "more excellent name" that Jesus inherits is essential to understanding His divine identity. In biblical theology, names are more than just labels; they convey essence and authority. The "more excellent name" is YHWH, a name that expresses God's eternal nature, sovereignty, and self-existence.

Verses 5 and 6 further illuminate this truth, with the author of Hebrews quoting Old Testament Scriptures originally addressed to YHWH and applying them to Jesus. Verse 5 reads, "For unto which of the angels said he at any time, Thou art my Son, this day have I begotten thee? And again, I will be to him a Father, and he shall be to me a Son?" This rhetorical question emphasizes Jesus' unique relationship with the Father, which no angel shares. God applies the quotations from Psalm 2:7 and 2 Samuel 7:14, which describe a father-son relationship, to Jesus, indicating His divine sonship and identity as YHWH.

Verse 6 continues, "And again, when he bringeth in the firstborn into the world, he saith, And let all the angels of God worship him." This verse alludes to Deuteronomy 32:43 (in the Septuagint) and Psalm 97:7, which exclusively direct worship towards God. The command for angels to worship Jesus emphasizes His divine status and is consistent with the reverence due to YHWH. The biblical context reserves worship for God, and this directive affirms Jesus' deity and His manifestation of the divine name.

These verses from Hebrews 1:4-6 establish a solid biblical foundation for the claim that Jesus Christ reveals YHWH in the New

Testament. The writer presents Jesus as the fulfillment and embodiment of YHWH's presence, power, and promise by inheriting a "more excellent name" and receiving worship that belongs solely to God. This understanding connects the Old and New Testaments, revealing the continuity of God's plan of salvation. Jesus, while distinct from the Father, shares the divine name YHWH, demonstrating the Godhead's profound unity and affirming the Christian confession of Jesus' identity and mission as God incarnate. This revelation deepens our understanding of Jesus, inviting us to appreciate the inseparable bond between Jesus and YHWH, as well as the ongoing story of redemption that God is telling through Him.

Pilate's Revelation

The inscription above Jesus' head on the cross, known as the "Titulus Crucis," reads "ישוע הנצרי ומלך היהודים" (Yeshua HaNazarei V'Melech HaYehudim), which translates to "Jesus of Nazareth, the King of the Jews" in English. This inscription, intended to denote the reason for Jesus' execution, unwittingly conceals an extraordinary connection to the divine name YHWH, a revelation with profound theological implications.

Hebrew - ישוע הנצרי ומלך היהודים (YHWH)
Greek - Ἰησοῦς ὁ Ναζωραῖος ὁ βασιλεὺς τῶν Ἰουδαίων (IHS)
Latin - IESVS NAZARENVS REX IVDÆORVM (INRI)

212

The Hebrew inscription contains an acronym formed by the first letters of each word: י (Yod) from ישוע (Yeshua), ה (Hey) from הנצרי (HaNazarei), ו (Vav) from ומלך (V'Melech), and ה (Hey) from היהודים (HaYehudim). These letters form יהוה (YHWH), the Tetragrammaton, the most sacred name of God in Judaism, indicating His eternal and self-existent nature. Derived from the declaration of Jesus' kingship and identity, this acronym serves as a powerful testimony to Jesus' divine nature and the fulfillment of Old Testament prophecies about the Messiah.

The presence of YHWH in the titulus crucis has significant implications. It implies that Jesus declares His identity as the embodiment of God on earth, even to the cross. It represents the divine orchestration of the crucifixion, in which the instrument of Jesus' humiliation becomes a declaration of His divine kingship and messianic mission. The crucifixion wasn't a tragedy; it was a victory.

This hidden revelation strengthens our faith in Jesus as the incarnate YHWH, the God of Israel, who came to dwell among His people and redeem them. It captures the paradox of the crucifixion, in which apparent defeat turns into God's ultimate victory over sin and death. Beyond its historical and immediate purpose, the Titulus Crucis serves as a profound theological statement, revealing YHWH's hidden but unmistakable presence in the crucifixion narrative and affirming Jesus' identity as the Messiah and the living breathing embodiment of the God of Israel, YHWH.

Cessation of YHWH

By the First-Century CE, there had been a significant shift in the use and pronunciation of the Tetragrammaton, YHWH, in Jewish religious practice. The Pharisaic interpretation of the third of the Ten Utterances commonly known to as the Ten Commandments, "You shall not take the name of the LORD your God in vain" (Exodus 20:7), influenced this renewed reverence for the divine Name, leading to the spoken use of HaShem. This evolving understanding highlighted a cautious approach to articulating God's sacred name, indicating a desire to avoid any potential misuse or disrespect.

The Tetragrammaton, YHWH, appears 6,828 times in the Hebrew Scriptures and is God's most sacred name, as revealed to Moses at the burning bush (Exodus 3:14). The High Priest only pronounced this name, symbolizing God's eternal existence and self-sufficiency, on special occasions like the Yom Kippur service in the Temple, as it was considered uniquely holy. However, following the Babylonian Exile and the loss of the Temple's central role in Jewish worship, YHWH's pronunciation became increasingly restricted, but not lost.

214

By the first century, the Temple, rebuilt but still adhering to the same reverent practices, no longer articulated the name YHWH in everyday speech or even in liturgical settings. Instead, name expressions such as "Adonai" (my Lord) and "HaShem" (The Name) were used. This practice demonstrated the Pharisees' and the wider Jewish community's dedication to upholding the sanctity of the divine name, preventing its careless or profane use, as understood to be mandated by the Third Utterance.

This change in practice significantly influenced the transmission and translation of the Hebrew Scriptures into the Greek Septuagint. The Septuagint translated the Tetragrammaton as "Kyrios" (Lord), mirroring the Jewish practice of reading "Adonai" instead of YHWH. The New Testament writings continue this translation choice, using "Kyrios" to refer to both Jesus and YHWH from the Old Testament, thereby reinforcing the connection between Jesus and the divine name in Christian doctrine.

The discontinuation of the use of YHWH and the adoption of substitute terms represent not only a cultural and religious shift, but also a deepening of theological understanding. During this period in Jewish history, reverence for the divine name led to a form of linguistic sanctification, preserving the sacredness of God's name by refraining from casual or irreverent use. Judaism and early Christianity approached, used, and interpreted the divine name with profound reverence and awe, using this historical and religious context as a backdrop.

I Am

Jesus' use of the phrase "I am" in the Gospels, particularly in relation to His identity and mission, is a profound exercise in self-identification that directly echoes the divine name that God gave to Moses at the burning bush—Ehyeh, translated as "I AM WHO I AM" (Exodus 3:14). God's self-designation, expressed as YHWH in Hebrew, embodies His eternal, self-existent nature, existing independently of all creation. When Jesus uses this phrase in the Gospel of John, He is not only identifying Himself; He is also invoking the divine name, making a bold statement about His own divine nature and oneness with the Father.

One of the most striking instances occurs in John 8:58, when Jesus declares, "Before Abraham was, I am." This statement not only confirms Jesus' preexistence but also His identity as the eternal God, directly aligning Himself with YHWH. His audience understood the significance of this claim; the Jewish leaders saw it as blasphemy, a man claiming to be God, and they sought to stone Him. For the believer, this incident should have screamed, "Look at me!" Compelling us to return to

216

the instance in which Jesus stated, "Your father Abraham rejoiced to see my day: and he saw it, and was glad." (John 8:56, KJV). What did Abraham see? Jesus stated that Abraham had witnessed "my day." This concept strikingly echoes to the "Day of the Lord," which is a period of dramatic transformation. It is a day of darkness, wrath, and terror for the unrighteous and those who have turned away from God, marking the execution of God's judgment on sin and rebellion. In contrast, for the faithful and righteous, the "Day of the LORD" represents hope, restoration, and salvation. Did Abraham see a day when God would judge the unrighteous and save the faithful? Yes! The destruction of Sodom led to the salvation of Lot. Interestingly, if we return to Genesis 19 and examine it through this lens, we discover something that, once seen, can't be unseen.

"The sun was risen upon the earth when Lot entered into Zoar. Then the LORD rained upon Sodom and upon Gomorrah brimstone and fire from the LORD out of heaven; And he overthrew those cities, and all the plain, and all the inhabitants of the cities, and that which grew upon the ground. But his wife looked back from behind him, and she became a pillar of salt. And Abraham gat up early in the morning to the place where he stood before the LORD: And he looked toward Sodom and Gomorrah, and toward all the land of the plain, and beheld, and, lo, the smoke of the country went up as the smoke of a furnace. And it came to pass, when

God destroyed the cities of the plain, that God remembered Abraham, and sent Lot out of the midst of the overthrow, when he overthrew the cities in the which Lot dwelt." (Genesis 19:23-29, KJV)

Did you see it? Did you catch the exact verse that Jesus wanted us to see? Look closely and slowly read, "**Then the LORD rained** upon Sodom and upon Gomorrah brimstone and fire / **from the LORD out of heaven;**" (Genesis 19:24). Amazingly, there are two LORDs given in this verse. The LORD on earth who caused it to rain brimstone on Sodom and Gomorrah, as did the other LORD from heaven. All of this makes even more sense when we consider that the two in Sodom and Gomorrah were not mere angels, as we may have previously assumed. They are, in fact, two of the three who appeared as the LORD in Genesis 18:1-2. This doubleness of LORD is not exclusive to Genesis 18 if we search carefully it happens over and over again throughout the Scriptures. One of the most interesting is found in Isaiah 48:16, where the LORD proclaiming to be the First and the Last (48:12) speaks and says, "Come ye near unto me, hear ye this; I have not spoken in secret from the beginning; from the time that it was, there am I: and now the Lord GOD, and his Spirit, hath sent me."

In John 10:22–42, Jesus' affirmation that "I and the Father are one" (John 10:30) reinforces this identification with the divine. Against the backdrop of the Feast of Dedication (Hanukkah), Jesus' statement elicited a violent reaction, challenging His Jewish contemporaries' strict monotheistic understanding by equating Himself with God. The charge of blasphemy and the subsequent attempt to stone Jesus highlight the radical nature of His claim to divine identity and authority. This does not imply that Jesus and the Father are synonymous; Jesus never claims the identity of the Father. Yet, it sheds light on His deep communion with the Father while underscoring their unique identities, as seen in John 17:1.

This assertion of oneness with the Father is consistent with the biblical concept of Shema, a foundational declaration of Jewish monotheism found in Deuteronomy 6:4. "Hear, O Israel: The LORD our God, the LORD is one (Echad)." The term "Echad," first mentioned when man cleaves unto his wife: and the two shall be one (echad) flesh, implies unity and oneness, implying a complex unity within the Godhead, as seen in the Hebrew word Elohim. Jesus' claim of oneness with the Father does not introduce a plurality of gods but rather affirms the complex unity of the one true God. This theological nuance is critical for understanding God's nature as revealed in the Scriptures, representing both unity and distinction within the Trinity.

"I Am" Statements

Jesus' "I am" statements are more than just claims to a special role or authority; they are direct invocations of the divine name, putting Him in the unique, self-existent nature of YHWH. These declarations connect the human and divine, providing profound insight into the mystery of the Incarnation: God becoming flesh in the person of Jesus Christ. Through Jesus, the eternal "I AM" enters human history, fulfilling God's promises and revealing the full extent of divine love and salvation. His audience's reactions, ranging from bewilderment to hostility, highlight the revolutionary nature of His identity and message, challenging us to wrestle with the implications of His divine lordship and invitation to know God through Him.

"I am the bread of life" (John 6:35, 48, 51): In contrast to the manna that the Israelites received in the desert, Jesus declares Himself to be the source of spiritual nourishment and eternal life, offering Himself as sustenance to satisfy the deepest hunger of the human soul. Exodus 16 describes YHWH providing manna from heaven to the Israelites in the wilderness, symbolizing God as the source of sustenance and life. Jesus, as the "bread of life," echoes this provision by offering Himself as the spiritual nourishment that leads to eternal life.

"I am the light of the world" (John 8:12; 9:5). Jesus claims to be the source of truth and enlightenment, leading humanity from the darkness of sin and ignorance into the light of understanding and righteous living. How is this a reference to YHWH? Psalm 27:1 states, "The LORD is my light and my salvation," identifying YHWH as a source of light who guides and delivers from darkness. Jesus' claim emphasizes His role in illuminating the way to God and freeing humanity from the darkness of sin.

"I am the door of the sheep" (John 10:7, 9): Jesus presents Himself as the only way to enter into a relationship with God, protecting His disciples as a shepherd does his flock. How is this a reference to YHWH? In Ezekiel 34:23–24, YHWH promises to appoint a single shepherd, David, to care for His flock. Jesus' statement I am the door echoes God's promise of leadership and protection for His people.

"I am the good shepherd" (John 10:11, 14): Building on the shepherd imagery, Jesus identifies Himself as the one who knows His sheep well and sacrifices Himself for their well-being, in contrast to the hired hand who abandons the sheep. Psalm 23 describes YHWH as the shepherd who leads, provides for, and protects His flock. Jesus identifies Himself as the good shepherd, emphasizing God's pastoral care and dedication to His people.

"I am the resurrection and the life" (John 11:25): Before raising Lazarus from the dead, Jesus asserts His authority over life and death and promises eternal life to those who believe in Him. How is this a reference to YHWH? In Ezekiel 37, YHWH revives the dry bones, symbolizing Israel's restoration and revival. Jesus' declaration connects Him to God's life-giving power, claiming authority over death and the promise of eternal life.

"I am the way, the truth, and the life" (John 14:6): Jesus makes a unique claim to be the only way to God, the embodiment of truth that sets people free, and the source of eternal life. While Psalm 25:5 refers to God as the "God of my salvation" and asks for guidance in the truth, Psalm 86:11 asks, "Teach me your way, O LORD." Jesus represents the ultimate revelation of God's way, truth, and provision for life.

"I am the true vine" (John 15:1, 5): Jesus describes Himself as the source of spiritual vitality and His disciples as branches that can bear fruit only if they stay connected to Him. How is this a reference to YHWH? Isaiah 5:1–7 refers to Israel as the LORD's vineyard, indicating YHWH's concern and expectation of fruitfulness from His people. Jesus, as the true vine, represents fulfillment, the true source of life and fruitfulness, in contrast to Israel's inability to produce righteousness.

The Ultimate Sacrifice

The name of God, YHWH (יהוה), has profound meanings that go beyond the surface as the sacred, ineffable name of the God of Israel. Consider the divine name in the context of the crucifixion narrative, especially in the Hebrew, Greek, and Latin inscription above Jesus' head on the cross, as recorded in John 19:19–20, to highlight its depth. Despite its seemingly straightforward nature, this act holds a much deeper prophetic revelation, directly linked to the name YHWH and Jesus' sacrificial act.

The Hebrew inscription "ישוע הנצרי ומלך היהודים" (Yeshua HaNazarei V'Melech HaYehudim), meaning "Jesus of Nazareth, the King of the Jews," as given previously in Pilate's Revelation, hides an acronym that reveals YHWH. The hidden presence of God's name in the declaration of Jesus' identity and kingship at the site of His crucifixion is not a coincidence but a divinely orchestrated revelation. It implies a strong link between Jesus' sacrificial death and YHWH's redemptive plan for humanity.

The chief priests' objection to Pilate's inscription, which they understood as a claim of kingship for Jesus, emphasizes this connection even more. Pilate's refusal to change the inscription, which reads "What I have written, I have written," emphasizes the significance of this event

223

and the divine purpose behind it. Pilate's decision, whether he knew it or not, ensured that the prophetic and messianic declarations remained, connecting Jesus directly to YHWH.

By leaving the inscription unchanged, Pilate unwittingly contributed to the revelation of Jesus as the embodiment of YHWH, the God of salvation. This event not only fulfilled Jewish messianic expectations, but it also revealed a deeper layer of God's salvific work in Jesus. Marked by the title "King of the Jews," the crucifixion becomes a theophany, announcing Jesus' identity as YHWH incarnate to all who could read the sign in Hebrew, Greek, and Latin, symbolizing the universal scope of His kingship and sacrifice.

The ancient Hebrew representation of the four pictograms of "YHWH" (יהוה) conceals much more:

- Yod (י): ᴗᴗ Symbolizing a hand, specifically a man's hand reaching upward or outward to grasp something, conveying the notions of work, throw, or worship.

- Hey (ה): ⵂ is the picture of a man with his arms raised meaning breath, behold, reveal.

- Vav (ו): Y Symbolizes a tent peg meaning to nail or to bind.

- Hey (ה): ⵂ is the picture of a man with his arms raised meaning breath, behold, reveal.

The divine name YHWH thus depicts the Hand Look! The Nail Look!

John uses this revelation as undoubtable proof of who Jesus is in John 20:27 when He said "Behold my hands!"

Thus, the inscription marking Jesus' crucifixion, which both proclaims His kingship and conceals the divine name YHWH, reveals the sacrificial nature of God's love. It bridges the Old Testament revelation of God's name with the New Testament revelation of God in Jesus, showing that the God who delivered Israel is the same God who brings salvation to all humanity through the cross. This profound integration of YHWH's name with Jesus' sacrificial act underscores the eternal and self-existing nature of Jesus from the very beginning, revealing the crucifixion as the culmination of God's redemptive plan unveiled through His divine name.

The Three

In Matthew 28:19, Jesus' Great Commission profoundly encapsulates the unity and distinct roles of the Father, the Son, and the Holy Ghost, instructing His disciples to baptize in "the name" (HaShem) of the Father, and of the Son, and of the Holy Ghost. The singular "name" mentioned invokes a deep theological significance, especially when viewed through the lens of Hebraic understanding, where "HaShem" serves as a reverent substitute for the Tetragrammaton, YHWH. And acting "in the name of" emphasizes the Godhead's authority and essence, signifying that this commission carries divine approval and power.

The singular usage of "the name" not "the names" in the Great Commission points to the threefold unity of the Godhead. This is not a call to recognize three distinct deities, but rather to recognize the oneness of God, manifested in three persons, each bearing the divine name YHWH in their distinct roles and relationships with humanity. The concept of "HaShem," which implies that the Father, the Son, and the Holy Spirit are cohesively active and present in the work of redemption and sanctification of believers, underscores this unity.

The baptism of Christ offers a vivid illustration of this threefold unity and distinction within the Godhead. As recounted in Matthew 3:16–17, all three persons are distinctly present at this pivotal moment: Jesus emerges from the water, the Holy Spirit descends in the form of a dove, and the Father's voice from heaven declares, "This is my beloved Son, in whom I am well pleased." This event not only validates Jesus' identity and mission but also showcases the distinct persons of the Trinity operating in perfect harmony, each bearing the divine name and authority of YHWH. The Great Commission mirrors the divine orchestration at Jesus' baptism, presenting a unified manifestation of the Father, the Son, and the Holy Ghost, each actively participating in the sacred act. Every baptism performed in the name of the Father, the Son, and the Holy Spirit is a replication of Jesus' own baptism.

Passages emphasizing the unified work of the Father, Son, and Holy Spirit, each bearing the name YHWH, provide further scriptural support for their shared divine authority in salvation and creation. For instance, Genesis 1:26 ("And God said, Let us make man in our image, after our likeness") explicitly presents the plural unity in the Godhead involved in creation, reflecting the shared divine essence. Additionally, John 10:30, where Jesus states, "I and my Father are one," reinforces the unity and shared authority within the Godhead, underpinning the Hebraic principle that actions taken "in the name of" invoke the full authority and essence of God. The stone that the builders refused further suggests the unity of Jesus and the Father. "The stone which the builders refused is become the head stone of the corner." (Psalm 118:22) Unbeknownst to the English reader, the word stone used here in Hebrew is eben (אֶבֶן). Amazingly, in this stone, we find yet another hidden message. The Stone אבן is father and son combined into one. Ab is the father, and Ben is son. To refuse one is to refuse them both because, as Jesus stated, "I and my Father are one." Jesus reemphasizes the very verse as the climax of the parable of the tenant in Mark 12:1-2 and *the Parable of the Wicked Husbandmen* (Matthew 21:33–46; Luke 20:9–18).

Stone אבן

Father אב | Son בן

Furthermore, the indwelling of the Holy Spirit, as promised by Jesus in John 14:26, "But the Comforter, which is the Holy Ghost, whom the Father will send in my name, he shall teach you all things," signifies the Spirit's role in guiding and empowering believers, acting "in the name" in the authority of Jesus and in the name of YHWH. This promise not only underscores the distinct roles within the Trinity but also the singular divine authority that they collectively embody.

Performing actions "in the name of" the Father, Son, and Holy Ghost calls believers to recognize and uphold the unity and authority of God as expressed in the distinct persons of the Trinity. Each person of the Godhead, bearing the divine name YHWH, participates in the redemptive work of God, inviting believers into a relationship characterized by the power, presence, and authority of the divine. The Great Commission, therefore, is not just a call to evangelize but a profound invocation of the triune God's authority and presence in the life of the believer and the mission of the Church.

The singular "the name" mentioned in Matthew 28:19, interpreted through the Hebraic concept of "HaShem" as a substitute for YHWH, reveals a deep theological truth about the unity and distinctiveness of the Father, the Son, and the Holy Ghost. Their presence at Jesus' baptism and the scriptural affirmations of their shared authority and essence highlight the threefold unity of the Godhead, each bearing the divine name YHWH. This understanding calls believers to acknowledge and act within the authority of the triune God, fulfilling the Great Commission with the assurance of the divine presence and power that accompanies the divine name.

Equal with God

Let this mind be in you, which was also in Christ Jesus: Who, being in the form of God, thought it not robbery to be equal with God: But made himself of no reputation, and took upon him the form of a servant, and was made in the likeness of men: And being found in fashion as a man, he humbled himself, and became obedient unto death, even the death of the cross. Wherefore God also hath highly exalted him, and given him a name which is above every name: That at the name of Jesus every knee should bow, of things in heaven, and things in earth, and things under the earth; And that every tongue should confess that Jesus Christ is Lord, to the glory of God the Father. (Philippians 2:5-11, KJV)

The profound declaration in Philippians 2:5–11 that Jesus Christ is equal with God offers theological insight into the nature of Christ and His intrinsic identity with YHWH, the sacred name of God. This passage, coupled with Jesus' own words in John 17, and the messianic prophecies in Psalms, collectively underscores Jesus' divinity and His embodiment of the name YHWH.

Philippians 2:5–11 encapsulates the mystery of Christ's divinity and humanity, highlighting His preexistence with God and voluntary humility in becoming human. "Who, being in the form of God, thought it not robbery to be equal with God: But made himself of no reputation, and took upon him the form of a servant, and was made in the likeness of men." This assertion of equality with God does not merely suggest a likeness in attributes or character but a profound unity in essence. The term "equal" here points to Jesus sharing the very nature and identity of God, thus implying that He, too, bears the divine name YHWH—the name that signifies eternal existence, sovereignty, and holiness.

In John 17:6, Jesus states, "I have manifested thy name unto the men which thou gavest me out of the world." This declaration during Jesus' prayer underscores His role in revealing the Father to humanity. The phrase "manifested thy name" takes on a heavy significance, indicating that Jesus made the nature and character of God known to His disciples. Given that "thy name" refers to YHWH, Jesus' statement suggests that through His words, actions, and very being, He has fully represented YHWH's essence to the world, affirming His divine status and unity with the Father.

Psalm 118:26, "Blessed be he that cometh in the name of the LORD," further supports the messianic identity of Jesus as bearing the name YHWH. This verse, quoted in the New Testament in the context of Jesus' triumphal entry into Jerusalem, aligns with the recognition of Jesus as the Messiah who comes in the authority and character of YHWH. The invocation of "the name of the LORD" here is not merely a reference to authority but to identity—Jesus comes as the embodiment of God's promises, the manifestation of YHWH to His people.

Moreover, Jesus' application of the divine name to Himself in John 8:58, where He declares, "Before Abraham was, I am," echoes the self-existence implied in the name YHWH, revealed to Moses in Exodus 3:14. This statement by Jesus, using the present tense "I am" to signify His eternal existence, directly correlates with the Tetragrammaton YHWH, meaning "He Who Is." Such a declaration is a clear assertion of Jesus' divinity and equality with God, as it directly invokes the sacred name associated with God's eternal, unchanging nature.

Additionally, Hebrews 1:3 beautifully encapsulates the divine identity and mission of Jesus, stating that He is "the brightness of his glory and the express image of his person." This description aligns with the understanding that Jesus is not only equal to God but is the exact representation of God's being, further underscoring His embodiment of the name YHWH. As the "express image" of God, Jesus manifests God's nature and character in the flesh, making the invisible God visible to humanity, hence Immanuel—God with us.

The revelation of God in Christ, as seen through these scriptural lenses, emphasizes that Jesus, equal with God, indeed bears the divine name YHWH. His mission to manifest the name of God, His fulfillment of messianic prophecies, and His declarations of eternal existence all point to His unique identity as God incarnate. The New Testament writers, drawing on Old Testament Scriptures and Jesus' own words, consistently portray Jesus as embodying the fullness of YHWH, bridging heaven and earth, and offering salvation to humanity.

One of the most overlooked aspects of Philippians 2:1–11 is its rich detail. "That at the name of Jesus every knee should bow, of things in heaven, and things in earth, and things under the earth; And that every tongue should confess that Jesus Christ is Lord, to the glory of God the Father." (Philippians 2:10–11, KJV). It is critical to remember that the phrase "the name of Jesus" is an idiom that captures His authority and essence. Every knee should bow before His exalted authority, whether in heaven, on earth, or beneath the earth. This revelation echoes the second of the words given in Exodus 20:4, "Thou shalt not make unto thee any graven image, or any likeness of any thing that is in heaven above, or that is in the earth beneath, or that is in the water under the earth." Equally overlooked is the confession. What will everyone who submits to Jesus' authority confess? He is Lord! The confession is not simply to identify Him as Jesus, nor is it that He is our Savior, the Messiah, the Son of Man, or the Son of God, but rather that He is Lord, YHWH!

The biblical narrative, which weaves through both Testaments, essentially presents a cohesive understanding of Jesus as equal with God, bearing the name YHWH. This unity in essence between the Father and the Son reveals the depth of God's love and the extent of His revelation to humanity through Jesus Christ. As we reflect on Jesus' identity and mission, we are invited into a deeper relationship with God, grounded in the recognition of Jesus as YHWH, the Savior, and Lord of all.

The LORD Said Unto My Lord

Psalm 110:1, "The LORD said unto my Lord, Sit thou at my right hand, until I make thine enemies thy footstool," spoken by David, introduces a profound theological dialogue that spans both the Old and New Testaments, culminating in the revelation of Jesus Christ as the embodiment of the name above all names, YHWH. This verse presents a fascinating dynamic within the Godhead, showcasing a conversation between two divine persons, and is foundational to understanding the messianic prophecy and its fulfillment in Jesus.

In the Hebrew text, "The LORD" is represented by the Tetragrammaton, YHWH, indicating the supreme, covenantal God of Israel. The phrase "unto my Lord" uses the word "Adonai," a term of respect and sovereign lordship. This distinction sets the stage for a messianic interpretation, where David, the king, acknowledges someone greater in authority and power than himself, pointing towards a future Messiah who holds a position of divine authority.

The New Testament revisits and emphasizes this verse, especially in Jesus' own teachings and the apostolic writings, to underscore Jesus' divine status and authority. For instance, Jesus references Psalm 110:1 in Matthew 22:41–46, Mark 12:35–37, and Luke 20:41–44 to question the Pharisees' understanding of the Messiah's nature, suggesting that the Messiah, being David's Lord, possesses a divine status.

Further, the New Testament identifies Jesus as the fulfillment of the messianic prophecy, the one who sits at the right hand of God, sharing in the divine authority and majesty of YHWH. Philippians 2:9–11 encapsulates this revelation, stating, "Wherefore God also hath highly exalted him, and given him a name which is above every name: That at the name of Jesus every knee should bow...and that every tongue should confess that Jesus Christ is Lord, to the glory of God the Father." This passage not only affirms Jesus' exaltation, but also identifies Him with the name above all names, implicitly connecting Him with YHWH, the ultimate declaration of His divinity and lordship.

The invocation of Psalm 110:1 in the New Testament, therefore, serves as a critical link between the Old Testament anticipation of a divine Messiah and the New Testament revelation of Jesus as the incarnate YHWH. It illustrates the continuity of God's redemptive plan, affirming Jesus' unique position within the Godhead and His role in the fulfillment of divine promises. Jesus reveals and manifests the name of YHWH in its full salvific power, underscoring the depth of His identity as "the name above all names" and solidifying His lordship and divine authority in the unfolding narrative of salvation history.

The Righteous Branch

In the grand unfolding of biblical revelation, the prophecy found in Jeremiah 23:1–8 and 33:14–16 stands as a monumental declaration of God's redemptive plan through a figure known as "the righteous Branch." This Branch, a descendant of David, is not merely a royal successor in the earthly sense but a divine embodiment of God's justice, righteousness, and salvation for His people. The profound declaration that this Branch shall be called "YHWH our Righteousness" encapsulates the essence of God's salvific work in history, merging the promises of old with the fulfillment found in Jesus Christ.

Jeremiah's prophecy emerges in a context of dire need for restoration and divine intervention. The LORD promised that if we call on Him, He will answer (Psalm 91:15; Jeremiah 33:3). Amidst the ruin of exile and the fragmentation of David's royal lineage, the promise of a righteous Branch who will execute judgment and justice brings hope of a renewed covenant and a restored kingdom. This Branch is not merely another king but the personification of YHWH's righteousness, embodying God's own character and bringing about salvation and justice.

The name "YHWH our Righteousness" attributed to this Branch is of the utmost significance. In the Hebrew Scriptures, righteousness is a hallmark of YHWH's character, denoting His faithfulness to the covenant and His commitment to the welfare of His people. By ascribing YHWH's name directly to the Branch, Jeremiah's prophecy indicates a deep unity between the Branch and YHWH Himself. This unity points beyond a representative or agent; the Branch is an embodiment of YHWH's righteousness, making God's salvific and just nature manifest in the world.

The New Testament reveals Jesus Christ as the fulfillment of Jeremiah's prophecy. The Gospels portray Jesus as the descendant of David who inaugurates God's kingdom, embodying justice, righteousness, and the very presence of God among His people. Through His life, teachings, death, and resurrection, Jesus fulfills the role of the righteous Branch, executing divine judgment and justice and establishing a new covenant in His blood.

The declaration of Jesus as "YHWH our Righteousness" finds its grounding in the reality of the Incarnation. Jesus, as God incarnate, bridges the divine and human, bringing about salvation and righteousness not through external adherence to the law but through a transformative relationship with God. Jesus fully fulfills the righteous requirements of the law, inviting humanity into the righteousness of God Himself. Faith in Christ bestows this righteousness as a gift of grace, not earned.

The implications of understanding Jesus as "YHWH our Righteousness" are transformative. This implies that Jesus reveals and makes accessible to humanity the fullness of God's character and salvific will. Salvation, therefore, is not merely a matter of judicial pardon but an invitation into the very life and righteousness of God. As believers we are not only declared righteous but are also made participants in the righteousness of Christ, which reshapes our lives, our relationships, and our engagement with the world.

Furthermore, this understanding deepens the Christian's appreciation of the unity within the Godhead. Jesus, as the righteous Branch, reveals the heart of the Father and accomplishes the work of the

237

Spirit. The triune God is actively involved in the work of redemption, with Jesus' incarnation serving as the pivotal moment in the divine narrative of salvation. Through Him, the promise of "YHWH our Righteousness" becomes a present reality, offering hope, transformation, and a foretaste of the coming kingdom.

Jeremiah's prophecy culminates in the revelation of Jesus as "YHWH our Righteousness." This is not merely a historical or theological curiosity. It is a vibrant and living truth that speaks to the heart of the Christian faith. It affirms that in Jesus, God has come close, offering His own righteousness to a world ensnared by sin and injustice. This divine act of grace invites believers to live in the light of God's righteousness, bearing witness to the hope and healing that come from knowing Jesus, the righteous Branch, as "YHWH our Righteousness."

The New Name

In the grand narrative of the Bible, name changes serve as milestones of transformation, destiny, and divine engagement. The transitions from Abram to Abraham, Sarai to Sarah, and Jacob to Israel each signify profound shifts in divine calling and purpose within the overarching story of God's interaction with humanity. Likewise, the New Testament recounts Simon's transformation into Peter, the foundational "rock" upon which the church stands. These name changes go beyond mere alteration of names; they signify a deep reshaping of identity and divine mission, reflecting each individual's pivotal role in the saga of redemption.

Saul to Paul

The transition from Saul to Paul in the Scriptures is not merely a change of name but a profound pivot in destiny and purpose, signifying a divine orchestration of identity that aligns with prophecy. This narrative journey begins with Saul of Tarsus, a figure initially introduced as a fervent persecutor of early Christians, whose encounter with Jesus on the Damascus Road marks a pivotal moment in biblical history and Christian theology. However, contrary to a common misconception, this encounter does not result in Jesus renaming Saul to Paul. Rather than a direct divine intervention in renaming, the transformation from Saul to Paul occurs subtly in the Acts of the Apostles, specifically in Acts 13:9.

This subtlety brings to light a critical understanding of biblical names, or "shems"—they encapsulate essence, destiny, and divine calling. Saul's transition to the name Paul does not follow the pattern of a divinely declared name change, unlike the dramatic name changes seen with patriarchs like Abram to Abraham or Jacob to Israel. Instead, it embodies a prophetic fulfillment, marking Saul's acceptance of a destiny that extends beyond his Hebrew roots to a global mission among the Gentiles.

And I will set a sign among them, and I will send those that escape of them unto the nations, to Tarshish, Pul, and Lud, that draw the bow, to Tubal, and Javan, to the isles afar off, that have not heard my fame, neither have seen my glory; and they shall declare my glory among the Gentiles. (Isaiah 66:19, KJV)

The name Paul, not inherently Hebrew and absent from Saul's Jewish lineage, intriguingly appears in the prophecy of Isaiah 66:19. This prophecy outlines God's plan to declare His glory among the nations, specifically mentioning Tarshish (the same as Tarsus), Pul (Paul), who would carry forth this divine revelation to the Gentiles. This connection between Saul of Tarsus and the prophecy emphasizes not a renaming of Saul but his embracing of a "name" that aligns with God's salvific outreach to all humanity, beyond the Jewish community.

The linguistic and prophetic threads weave a compelling narrative where Saul, the once zealous Pharisee, becomes Paul, the apostle to the Gentiles. This transformation is more than a change of name; it's a redirection of life's purpose, underpinned by divine ordination. Saul's journey and his acceptance of the name Paul illustrate the biblical theme that names hold power and destiny. They are not arbitrary tags but divine markers of one's role in the unfolding story of redemption.

But the Lord said unto him, Go thy way: for he is a chosen vessel unto me, to bear my name before the Gentiles, and kings, and the children of Israel: For I will shew him how great things he must suffer for my name's sake. (Acts 9:15–16, KJV)

Paul's mission, as foretold by Isaiah and affirmed by Jesus' directive to Ananias in Acts 9:15–16, is a testament to the intricate ways God's plans are revealed and realized through individuals' lives. Paul, an apostle born out of time, embodies the fulfillment of a divine promise to extend salvation's reach beyond Israel to every nation, tribe, and tongue.

This narrative underscores the profound impact of a "name" shift —how a name, or rather the acceptance of a specific calling and identity, can steer one's destiny towards fulfilling God's overarching plan. Saul's acceptance of being called Paul signifies his alignment with a prophetic destiny, marking a transition from persecutor to principal proclaimer of the gospel to the Gentiles. Through Paul, we witness the unfolding of God's redemptive plan, a plan that transcends time, culture, and language, affirming that in the economy of divine purpose, names are far more than mere identifiers; they are divine beacons guiding the path to fulfilling God's will on earth.

Our Savior's New Name

The narrative arc that leads to Jesus receiving a "new" name occupies a unique and profoundly theological space within this tradition. Unlike the name changes experienced by Abraham, Sarah, Jacob, Peter, and even that of Saul to Paul, which all indicated changes in earthly mission and identity, the new name bestowed upon Jesus in Philippians 2:9–11 heralds the reaffirmation and unveiling of His eternal identity and divine sovereignty. Keep in mind that the Apostle Paul is directly quoting and reemphasizing ideas revealed in Isaiah 45:23. This passage elucidates that God has highly exalted Jesus, giving Him "the name that is above every name." Jesus' incarnation, crucifixion, and resurrection reveal this name afresh and reinstate it in its full magnificence, far from being novel in the chronological sense.

Compare Isaiah 45:23 and Philippians 2:10–11

"I have sworn by myself, the word is gone out of my mouth in righteousness, and shall not return, That unto me every knee shall bow, every tongue shall swear." (Isaiah 45:23, KJV)

"That at the name of Jesus every knee should bow, of things in heaven, and things in earth, and things under the earth; And that every tongue should confess that Jesus Christ is Lord, to the glory of God the Father." (Philippians 2:10–11, KJV)

Although not explicitly mentioned in Philippians, Isaiah Chapter 45 reveals that the "me" in "unto me every knee shall bow, every tongue shall swear" is the supreme name of YHWH. This sacred name, revealed to Moses, signifies the eternal, self-sufficient nature of God. Jesus, in His life and teachings, fully embodies and manifests the authority and essence of YHWH. He breathes life into the divine name in ways previously concealed through His unity with the Father, His role in creation, and His work of redemption.

YHWH, a name encapsulating God's self-existence and immutable nature, echoes through Jesus' declarations of "I am" in the Gospel of John, affirming His divinity, preexistence, and eternal unity with the Father. The "new" name given to Jesus thus represents not an introduction of a novel designation but the restoration and revelation of His divine status, previously veiled during His ministry on earth.

Furthermore, this exalted name signifies Jesus' dominion over all creation, His triumph over sin and death, and His mediatorial role between God and humanity. This name embodies His redemptive mission, His kingship, and the fulfillment of messianic prophecies, unveiling Jesus as the ultimate manifestation of God. The fullness of deity becomes tangible through Jesus (Colossians 2:9), reconciling all creation to God (Colossians 1:20).

In the realm of biblical tradition, names wield the power to convey essence, purpose, and destiny. The conferral of the name above all names upon Jesus is not merely a ceremonial honor but a declaration of His central role in the divine plan of redemption. It underscores the uniqueness of Christ's nature and mission, setting apart His name from those of the patriarchs and apostles. Their transformations marked new chapters in their earthly journeys, but Jesus' name encapsulates the unveiling of God's eternal purpose and presence.

The intent of this book is not to diminish the profound significance of the name Jesus; rather, it aims to illuminate its depth within the context of the triune missional roles of our God incarnate— Lord, Savior, Messiah. Jesus embodies these roles, manifesting as YHWH our Savior and Messiah—King, Priest, and Prophet. Each name unveils a facet of His divine mission, offering a richer understanding of His identity and the multifaceted way He engages with humanity and creation. This perspective elevates our appreciation of Jesus, not just as a name, but as the fulfillment of God's redemptive plan through His roles as our sovereign Lord, redeeming Savior, and eternal Messiah.

This "new" name, therefore, stands as both a revelation and a reaffirmation, asserting Jesus' timeless identity as Immanuel, God with us, the Messiah who saves, and the sovereign Lord of all. This profound truth culminates the biblical story, revealing the heart of God, His redemptive intent, and His sovereign rule over history. Jesus not only discloses but also makes YHWH accessible, inviting everyone into a dynamic relationship with the God of love, the Redeemer, and the eternal King. This climactic revelation calls for a response of worship and allegiance, recognizing Jesus as the definitive expression of YHWH, the Name above all names, inviting all of creation into the embrace of the God who was, who is, and who is to come.

In this elucidation of divine revelation, our Lord Jesus Christ represents the ultimate consummate, the fulfillment of God's eternal plan to reveal the glory of His name, YHWH. Jesus' incarnation, crucifixion, and resurrection reduce the infinite to finite, bring the eternal into time, and make the transcendent God tangible to the human experience.

When we look at Christ's glorious majesty, we see the convergence of the divine and the human, the eternal and the temporal, the Creator and the created. Jesus fully expresses the ineffable name of YHWH, shattering human comprehension and inviting us into a realm of awe-inspiring wonder.

Jesus' identity as YHWH, yet distinct from the Father and from the Holy Spirit, reveals an intricate web that weaves divine love, redemption, and sovereignty into the very fabric of reality. Through His life, death, and resurrection, Jesus invites us to embrace the incomprehensible mystery of the Godhead and to meet the living, breathing essence of YHWH in all of His transformative power.

We must respond to this profound revelation with hearts filled with worship, reverence, and surrender. For in the name above all names, we find the universe's very heartbeat, the eternal rhythm of love and grace that echoes throughout time. In Jesus, we see the face of the Almighty, the expressed image of God, the fullness of the Godhead, the Redeemer, who invites us into the embrace of the triune God, where we discover our true identity, purpose, and eternal hope.

Let this profound understanding draw us into an intimate relationship with Jesus, recognizing Him not just as our savior alone but as YHWH incarnate. As we delve deeper into the mysteries of His divine essence, let us become vessels through which His boundless love flows, echoing the harmony of creation's grand symphony. For in the name above all names lies not only the key to our salvation but an invitation to journey into the heart of God, where infinite grandeur unfolds. This journey with Jesus inheriting and given the name YHWH is an adventure into the eternal, a call to live in the fullness of divine love, and to manifest that love in every facet of our existence.

We stand at the threshold of the divine, enveloped by the mystery and splendor of God, in the revelations that Jesus received a name that is above every name (Philippians 2:9) and by inheritance obtained a more excellent name than the angels (Hebrews 1:4), the name YHWH. This revelation beckons us into an awe-inspiring realm of worship and reshapes our lives with the touch of His eternal presence.

Chapter Twelve

THE GODHEAD

T he awe-inspiring doctrine of the Trinity is central to Christianity, an enigmatic beacon that reveals God as a single essence manifesting in three distinct persons: the Father, the Son, and the Holy Spirit, all known by the same name (Matthew 28:19). While distinct in personhood, the sacred name YHWH unites this divine trio, expanding our understanding of God's nature and the profound interconnectedness of the Godhead.

The Shared Name

It is impossible to overstate the significance of the Father, Son, and Holy Spirit sharing the name YHWH. This shared name is more than a label; it expresses the divine essence, embodying God's unity, power, and eternal presence. It is a profound statement of their indivisible nature and collective lordship over all creation, bridging the gap between the unknown and the known, the infinite and the intimate.

In the fabric of biblical revelation, the Trinitarian Persons' relationship with the name YHWH reveals a dynamic interplay of relation, identity, and mission. This divine name, revered and proclaimed in the Hebrew tradition, transcends human categories, inviting us to a deeper contemplation of God as three yet one. The Father, Son, and Holy Spirit, while distinct in their relational roles and interactions, share an undeniably divine essence, encapsulated in the sacred tetragrammaton YHWH.

Scripture reflects God's mystery and majesty through the profound motif of threeness. Notably, YHWH's appearance to Abraham as three men in Genesis 18 foreshadows the Trinity concept, implying a divine communion beyond human comprehension. Moses received the name "Ehyeh Asher Ehyeh" ("I Am That I Am"), a triadic expression of God's self-existence, eternity, and sufficiency.

Interestingly, each word in the sacred name "Ehyeh Asher Ehyeh" revealed to Moses by YHWH begins with the letter Aleph, the first letter of the Hebrew alphabet and a symbol for the number one, resulting in a sequence of 1-1-1. This is not a linguistic coincidence but rather a profound example of unity and individuality encapsulated in the divine name YHWH. The spelling of Aleph's letters אלפ–Aleph (1), Lamed (30), and Pey (80), add up to 111, symbolizing the unity of three distinct entities that are also one.

אלפ (Aleph)

80 + 30 + 1 = 111

This divine revelation to Moses contains a hidden but magnificent reflection of YHWH's divine essence—unity in diversity. Each '1' in the sequence stands alone but is inextricably linked, providing a glimpse into the profound mystery and majesty of YHWH's nature, as revealed by the very name given to Moses. This layered meaning within "Ehyeh Asher Ehyeh" beautifully emphasizes YHWH's intricate unity, inviting reflection on the oneness and plurality that define the divine being.

The seraphim in Isaiah 6 further echo this thematic occurrence of threes in their celestial proclamation "Holy, Holy, Holy," a triple exaltation that highlights God's supreme holiness and otherness across time dimensions—past, present, and future. Why Holy, Holy, Holy? Why not just Holy? The thrice repeated "Holy, Holy, Holy" could suggest recognition of the divine Trinity, as described in 1 John 5:7, where "there are three that bear record in heaven, the Father, the Word, and the Holy Ghost, and these three are one." This interpretation could indicate that the early Christians understood each holy as an acknowledgement of God's triune nature, with each member being equally Holy.

Furthermore, the plural form of many Hebrew names for God, ending in "-im" (for example, "Elohim"), implies a multiplicity that traditionally emphasizes three or more, which is consistent with God's trinitarian nature.

The narrative of Scripture, enriched by the use of "Elohim" and "Adonai," subtly but powerfully emphasizes this composite unity. The plural form "Elohim," combined with singular verbs, and the sovereign title "Adonai" reflect the complexity and unity of God's essence.

Through these linguistic nuances, the Scriptures allude to a single divine essence that encompasses a number of individuals, each bearing the name YHWH and participating in the divine will and work. This plurality not only represents majesty and power, but it also implies the intricate unity of the divine essence. These examples, among others, serve as scriptural harmonics, resonating with the divine's threeness theme and inviting believers to delve deeper into the triune God's nature and revelation throughout the biblical narrative.

John's Gospel, particularly Chapter 17, provides a compelling examination of this unity. Jesus emphasizes the pre-incarnate glory He shares with the Father in His prayer, "with the glory I had with you before the world began," firmly anchored in the shared name of YHWH. This moment not only emphasizes Jesus' divinity, but it also demonstrates the Godhead's eternal fellowship and unity.

United

The Hebraic concept of "echad," which means unity or oneness, illuminates the Godhead's relationship under the name YHWH. The Shema's declaration of the Lord's oneness (Deuteronomy 6:4) exemplifies this unity, which does not eliminate distinctions within the Godhead, but rather affirms a complex unity that shares the divine essence and mission. Jesus' invocation of "echad" in His prayer reflects not only believers' unity but also divine oneness, inviting humanity into YHWH's sacred fellowship.

The shared divine name serves as the foundation of Trinitarian doctrine, emphasizing God's relational, sovereign, and redemptive nature. It reveals a God who, in His very being, exemplifies perfect unity and diversity, inviting believers to gain a deeper understanding of His nature and desire for relationship with His creation. The Trinity reveals a God who is complex in unity and coherent in diversity, transcendent in majesty but immanent in love—all unified under the name YHWH.

Furthermore, our Lord Jesus Christ reveals His divinity not through explicit declarations, but through His actions and words that align with the identity of YHWH. When Jesus says, "I am," He aligns Himself with the eternal God of Israel, bridging temporal existence and divine eternity. Jesus strengthens His position as YHWH, embodying the shared divine essence with the Father and the Holy Spirit, each time He aligns with God's identity, accepts worship, and proclaims unity with the Father.

The early church's doctrinal clarifications, resulting from councils and scriptural exegesis, firmly rooted Jesus' divine nature and the Holy Spirit's personhood in the shared essence of YHWH. These developments highlight the Godhead's inseparable unity and distinct personhood, a mystery that serves as the foundation for Christian faith and worship.

In essence, the Father, Son, and Holy Spirit share the name YHWH, which is a divine reality that invites believers into the heart of God's eternal mystery. It is a testimony to the God who desires to be known, loved, and worshiped as one God, in three Persons, each fully God and bearing the name YHWH, inviting us into a dynamic relationship with the Creator, Redeemer, and Sustainer of all. This profound mystery calls us to deeper worship, more profound prayer, and a life transformed by the love and power of the one true God (Elohim Echad Amiti), YHWH, in all of His glory.

This unity under the name YHWH is more than just a theological declaration; it is a transformative reality that affects all aspects of Christian life and worship. Scripture reveals God's identity and mission, deeply rooted in our relationship with the shared divine name. It emphasizes that the Father, Son, and Holy Spirit are coequally and eternally engaged in the work of creation, redemption, and sanctification, all under the majestic banner of YHWH.

Worship and Relationship

The Godhead's shared name, YHWH, deepens our understanding of salvation as a unified narrative flowing from God's heart. From the covenant promises of the Old Testament to Jesus' life, death, and resurrection, as well as the outpouring of the Holy Spirit, we see the triune God working together to restore creation to its original glory. This divine synergy emphasizes the consistency of God's nature and purposes throughout history, revealing the depth of God's love and the scope of His plan for humanity.

This understanding transforms our approach to worship, guiding us to honor the Trinity's shared essence as YHWH rather than individual persons. Our songs, prayers, and liturgies become expressions of worship for a God who is both three and one, recognizing each Person's distinct contributions while celebrating their unity. This perspective enriches our spiritual lives by providing a more nuanced and profound encounter with the divine.

Recognizing the Trinity's shared name also strengthens prayer. The Holy Spirit draws us into YHWH's divine communion as we address the Father through the Son. Our prayers become a part of the eternal conversation within the Godhead, a privilege that deepens our relationship with God and transforms our understanding of what it means to communicate with and hear from the divine.

Furthermore, the recognition of the Trinity's unified purpose under the name YHWH strengthens the church's mission. The church's call to make disciples, serve the poor, and proclaim the gospel stems from the triune God's mission to reconcile all things to Himself. Understanding this dynamic unity empowers us to embark on this mission with a sense of purpose and power, knowing that we are contributing to YHWH's ongoing work in the world.

The doctrine of the Trinity, encapsulated in the shared name YHWH, serves as both a beacon of hope and a source of mystery. It calls us to a faith founded on the revelation of God's nature as three-in-one, inviting us to delve into the depths of God's being and live out the implications of this truth in all aspects of life. It challenges us to embrace the mystery of the Godhead as a reality to be lived rather than a problem to be solved—a reality that reveals God's love for His creation and His desire for a relationship with us.

The shared name YHWH represents the ultimate expression of unity and diversity, a divine paradox that speaks to the very core of existence. It takes us on a journey of discovery, where faith and reason, worship and wonder, service and sacrifice, are all intertwined in the divine dance of the Trinity. As we delve deeper into the Trinity's mystery, we are transformed by YHWH's love, power, and presence, bringing us closer to God's heart and empowering us to reflect His triune nature in a world in need of His grace and truth.

In this journey with our triune God, we are constantly reminded that the essence of our faith is found not in abstract doctrines but in the living relationship we are invited to with YHWH. The Three reveal a God who is personal, relational, and endlessly loving, providing us with a profound and transformative vision of divine life. Living in the light of the Trinity calls us to embody this divine relationship in our daily lives, demonstrating YHWH's unity, love, and glory in a world yearning for redemption and hope.

The LORD is Our Savior

In the crowning glory of *The Name Above All Names*, we rediscovered the profound truth that has echoed through the corridors of faith, transcending ordinary language or tradition. When we use the name "Lord" Jesus Christ, we are not simply following a tradition or invoking a title; rather, we are acknowledging the fullness of His divine identity and authority. It's a declaration of His lordship, His role as Savior, and His exalted position as the Anointed One, the Messiah. This name encapsulates the essence of His mission, His power to save, and His rightful place as the "King of kings and Lord of lords" (1Timothy 6:15).

Scripture deeply weaves an ancient and sacred affirmation into our lives, often leaving us unaware of its rich implications. Greek scholars reverently substituted the term "Kyrios," translated as "Lord," for the Tetragrammaton, YHWH, God's sacred and unutterable name. This substitution stemmed from a deep reverence for the Divine Name, which was too holy for mortal utterance, and served to connect the Hebrew Scriptures to Greek-speaking Jews and early Christian followers.

As a result, the salutation "Lord Jesus Christ" represents a theological declaration rooted in YHWH's divine mystery rather than mere respect. This name establishes a timeless connection between the God of Israel and the Messiah, Jesus Christ. "Lord" (Kyrios) becomes a direct gateway to YHWH, implying that addressing Jesus as "Lord" (YHWH) acknowledges His divine essence and inseparable union with the God of the Hebrew Scriptures.

This composite name "Lord Jesus Christ" unfolds as the most profound proclamation of faith: YHWH Yeshua Mashiyach, or "YHWH, is the anointed Savior," further enriched by the Hebrew name Yeshua, meaning "The LORD is salvation," and the title "Christ" or "Mashiyach," signifying the anointed one. This linguistic and theological fusion solidifies our faith in Jesus as the prophesied Messiah who fulfills Old Testament prophecies and as God incarnate, central to the divine mission.

Thus, the name "Lord Jesus Christ" is more than just a conventional or ritualistic utterance. It is a powerful declaration of Jesus' identity as YHWH, confirming His divine role in the Godhead and His mission as the anointed savior and king. When we proclaim Him "Lord," we acknowledge and celebrate the profound truth of His divine nature, as well as the fulfillment of God's redemptive narrative through Him.

Even in the midst of these revelations, there remains an intriguing mystery, as hinted at in Revelation 2:17. Just as we anticipate receiving a unique name known only to ourselves and God, Jesus has a name no man knows (Revelation 19:12). This enigmatic name represents the pinnacle of divine revelation, proclaiming Jesus, YHWH is Salvation, as the ultimate authority. The name "Lord Jesus Christ" already goes beyond convention and serves as a powerful affirmation of His divine nature and redemptive mission as YHWH, YHWH's salvation, and the Anointed One —King, Prophet and Priest. However, this name represents the culmination of God's plan, the fulfillment of His promises, and the climax of history, contained within this grand unveiling of a name that remains hidden and holds within it the ultimate revelation.

Consider this intriguing possibility. According to Proverbs 25:2, "It is the glory of God to conceal a thing: but the honour of kings is to search out a matter." Could this be a hint from the divine? In Revelation 19:16, the title "KING OF KINGS AND LORD OF LORDS" is written in Hebrew as מלך המלכים ואדני האדנים. To discover this name, it is vital that we recognize the importance of the role that acrostics have played throughout this book as given in the Bible, from the revelation of the name Yah to the giving of the name Ehyeh Asher Ehyeh concealing 111, and Pilate's Titulus Crucis, reading Yeshua HaNazarei V'Melech HaYehudim, revealing the most sacred name YHWH. If we follow this very same biblical pattern for KING OF KINGS AND LORD OF LORDS, using the first letter of each word, we get מהוה, in English, MHWH. Astoundingly revealing yet another layer to the names Ehyeh (אהיה) and YHWH (יהוה), now embodied as Mehaveh (מהוה).

מֶלֶךְ הַמלכים וַאדני הָאדנים
מהוה

In "Mehaveh," the prefix "Mem" (מ) signifies "from" or "to come from," while "Havah" (הוה) is the past tense form of "to be," indicating events or existence in the past. Thus, Mehaveh means "to create" or "to bring into being"—the Creator. Although this name does not explicitly refer to creation, which in Hebrew is beriah (בריאה), it reaches beyond it to unveil the act of creating in the sense of bringing forth something from nothing, ex nihilo. MHWH deepens our understanding and further enhances John's revelation with a new found clarity, "All things were made by him; and without him was not any thing made that was made." (John 1:3, KJV)

This discovery heightens the significance of the implicit connection of the name above all names, YHWH, now given a new dimension, Mehaveh, to Jesus, albeit in a new form, MHWH.

Ehyeh אהיה - I am / I was / I will be
Yehovah / Yahweh יהוה - He caused to be
Mehaveh מחוה - To bring into being

Could all of this be a coincidence? Impossible!

The revelations in this book invite all believers to embark on a journey of discovery and contemplation. They offer only a glimpse of the profound depths concealed within God's Word, urging us to delve deeper. *The Name Above All Names* only hints at the vast treasures that await those who seek God's hidden wisdom in reverence and awe.

But don't take my word for it...

(Scan QR Code)

VideoTeachings

Other Books
Elucidations

God's Garden